The Noble Spanish Soldier by Thomas Dekker

Thomas Dekker was a playwright, pamphleteer and poet who, perhaps, deserves greater recognition than he has so far gained.

Despite the fact only perhaps twenty of his plays were published, and fewer still survive, he was far more prolific than that. Born around 1572 his peak years were the mid 1590's to the 1620's – seven of which he spent in a debtor's prison. His works span the late Elizabethan and Caroline eras and his numerous collaborations with Ford, Middleton, Webster and Jonson say much about his work.

His pamphlets detail much of the life in these times, times of great change, of plague and of course that great capital city London a swirling mass of people, power, intrigue.

Index of Contents
THOMAS DEKKER – AN INTRODUCTION
HISTORY OF THE NOBLE SPANISH SOLDIER ('NSS')
Text
Sources, Authorship and Date
Performance
ACTION OF THE PLAY
EDITORIAL PRACTICE
DRAMATIS PERSONAE
THE PRINTER TO THE READER
ACT THE FIRST
SCENE I
SCENE II
ACT THE SECOND
SCENE I
ACT THE THIRD
SCENE I
SCENE II
SCENE III
ACT THE FOURTH
SCENE I
SCENE II
ACT THE FIFTH
SCENE I
THOMAS DEKKER – A SHORT BIOGRAPHY
THOMAS DEKKER – A CONCISE BIBLIOGRAPHY

THOMAS DEKKER – AN INTRODUCTION

Thomas Dekker is believed to have been born in London around 1572, but nothing is known for certain about his youth. He embarked on a career as a theatre writer early in his adult life, the first extant text of his work being 'Old Fortunatus' written around 1596, although there are plays connected with his name which were performed as early as 1594. The period from 1596 to 1602 was the most prolific of his career, with 20 plays being attributed to him and an involvement in up to 28 other plays being suggested. It was during this period that he produced his most famous work, 'The Shoemaker's Holiday, or the Gentle Craft', categorised by modern critics as citizen comedy, it reflects his concerns with the daily lives of ordinary Londoners. This play exemplifies his vivid use of language and the intermingling of everyday subjects with the fantastical, embodied in this case by the rise of a craftsman to Mayor and the involvement of an unnamed but idealised king in the concluding banquet.

He exhibited a similar vigour in such prose pamphlets as the ironically entitled 'The Wonderfull Yeare' (1603), about the plague, 'The Belman of London' (1608), about roguery and crime, and 'The Guls Horne-Booke' (1609), a valuable account of behaviour in the London theatres.

Dekker was partly responsible for devising the street entertainment to celebrate the entry of James I into London in 1603 and he managed the Lord Mayor's pageant in 1612. His fortunes took a turn for the worse shortly after, when between 1613 and 1619 he was imprisoned, probably for debt; this experience may be behind his six prison scenes first included in the sixth edition (1616) of Sir Thomas Overbury's 'Characters'. He died in 1632 and was buried at St James', Clerkenwell.

HISTORY OF THE NOBLE SPANISH SOLDIER ('NSS')

Text

The first clear reference to the play is dated as 16 May 1631 when an entry was made in the Stationer's Register, effectively licensing texts for publication. The entry, made for John Jackman, referred to manuscripts of two plays by 'Tho: Dekker', these being 'The Wonder of a Kingdom' and 'a Tragedy called The Noble Spanish Soldier'. A similar entry was made on 9 December 1633, this time for Nicholas Vavasour. The play was printed in a quarto version in 1634, probably by John Beale, on behalf of Vavasour, who initialled the foreword entitled 'The Printer to The Reader'.

Sources, Authorship and Date

These aspects of the play have attracted more critical attention than all others combined, reference frequently being made to the following known facts:

(1) Although the entries in the Stationer's Register refer unambiguously to Dekker as the author, the title page of the Quarto states that the play is written by 'S.R.', the only Jacobean playwright with those initials being Samuel Rowley.

(2) It has been observed, initially by nineteenth century scholar A. H. Bullen, that three sections of a play by John Day called 'The Parliament of Bees' are nearly identical to sections of NSS. Furthermore a further five sections correspond closely to parts of 'The Wonder of a Kingdom' which as is noted above, was registered alongside NSS in 1931.

(3) In 1601, theatre manager Philip Henslow made part payment for an anonymous play called 'The Spanish Fig', no text of which survives under that name.

(4) In April 1624 a poster appeared in Norwich advertising a touring play, being 'An excellent Comedy called The Spanish Contract' to be performed by Lady Elizabeth's men, a company with which Dekker is believed to have had connections.

(5) There is some evidence of confusion in how the play has been compiled for printing, in particular, a cast list which omits several significant characters, the late appearance of two pointless characters (Signor No and Juanna) and the delayed identification of Alanzo as Captain of the Guard. These have been argued to be evidence of revision of an earlier work.

(6) Dekker's 'The Welsh Embassador' reworked much of the material in NSS, albeit in a comedic form. This is generally dated as c1623.

As may be imagined, these facts offer a considerable range of possibilities as to authorship and provenance of the play. Various critics, such as Fleay and Bullen, have tried to make sense of all of them by postulating, largely without evidence, a variety of permutations of collaboration and revision so as to give all of the authorship candidates a role in the production of the text we now have. The most persuasive contribution however, comes from Julia Gasper who, building on work by R. Koeppel, convincingly identifies the source of NSS as being Volume V of Jacques-Auguste de Thou's Latin 'Historiarum Sui Temporis', published in 1620.

The de Thou volume tells of how Henri IV of France reneged on a written promise of marriage to Hentiette d'Entragues, by marrying Marie be Medicis in 1600; both women bore sons by the King, who is later assassinated. This closely anticipates the marriage plot of NSS but the critical detail which seals the identification of de Thou as the source, is his reference to a soldier called Balthazare Sunica who acted against the King and was clearly, the original of the character Balthazar in NSS. This evidence demonstrates that the earliest date for composition of NSS is 1620. Furthermore, due to the likelihood that NSS predated 'The Welsh Embassador' of 1623/4, a last possible date for the writing of NSS, can also be deduced and a composition date of around 1622 can be established with some certainty.

With respect to the relationship with other plays, any connection with the 'The Spanish Fig' would seem to be ruled out on the grounds that it pre-dates the publication of de Thou's Historiarum. In the case of the later play 'The Spanish Contract', a connection is possible although any theories that may be advanced little more than conjecture. One such theory, put forward by Tirthanker Bose, is that 'the Spanish Contract' is a version of NSS, reworked as a comedy and thus is an intermediate stage on the road to 'The Welsh Embassador'.

The more pressing matter, the question of the connection with 'The Parliament of Bees', is also addressed by Julia Gasper. The crucial evidence here relates to instances where details, meaningful only in the context of NSS, have become embedded in the text of 'The Parliament of Bees'. The most significant example of this occurs in Scene 1, Line 29 of 'The Parliament of Bees' where a character asks 'Is Master Bee at leisure to speak Spanish / With a Bee of Service?'. There is no connection between 'The Parliament of Bees' and Spain or indeed, the Spanish language, so it would seem strong evidence that NSS was the source for 'The Parliament of Bees' and not the other way around. This evidence is supplemented by an analysis of NSS, Act 2 Scene 1, a scene common to both plays, when Balthazar sets out his credentials of loyal service in seeking to advise the King. Gasper points out that this scene in NSS contains elements from de Thou, not to be found in The Parliament of Bees, principally the need to intervene on behalf of Onaelia. The only plausible order of composition for the plays therefore places NSS before 'The Parliament of Bees'. Furthermore as Day's name has never been associated with NSS, there is no reason to suppose he was involved in its composition. The likelihood is therefore that he was lifting dialogue from an earlier work by another writer in order to serve his own convenience.

The remaining question to be considered concerns the relative claims to authorship of Dekker and Rowley. In weighing the evidence, it is important to consider that that the first records, those on the Stationer's Register, unequivocally record Dekker as the sole author. Furthermore, textual scholarship is happy to place NSS within the Dekker cannon, while, as Hoy says 'no scholar has ever succeeded in demonstrating Rowley's share in the play'. Given that is has been established that the play post-dates 1620, the possibility of a Dekker revision of an earlier Rowley text would appear to be implausible. The attribution to 'S.R.' remains unexplained, although it may be noted in passing that the initials are the final letters of Dekker's names, so it may just be a coded reference to Dekker. More likely perhaps, it could be the result of the editorial confusion which also pervades the compilation of the cast list.

Performance

There is no firm record of the play being performed, although the foreword does make mention of it being enthusiastically received. Such references are not, of course, to be taken at face value as they would hardly be expected to say anything else; nevertheless, it does strongly suggest that the play has been staged. In practice, the printing of a text suggests either high popularity, in which case sales could be expected to compensate for possible plagiarism, or else relative unpopularity in which case publication was a last attempt to generate some financial return before the play was discarded. In this instance, the later circumstance is likely to obtain, especially in view of the gap between writing and publication dates.

ACTION OF THE PLAY

The sub-title given to the text in the Quarto edition is 'A contract Broken, Justly Revenged'. Although this title is likely to have been added by the printers, it does succinctly sum up one aspect the play, the theme of revenge which is reminiscent of Elizabethan revenge plays such as Thomas Kidd's 'The Spanish Tragedy'. Revenge plays however, are generally patterned around a revenger and what may be termed a 'revengee', while the action of NSS revolves around a power struggle between two factions both of whom are concerned with violent intent. In reality, the play reflects the seventeenth century fashion for mixing elements of tragedy and comedy in a style first identified by Sir Philip Sydney in 1579 as being 'mongrel tragicomedy'; thus while death intrudes on the final act, it only strikes unsympathetic characters. There is also regular light relief provided by two comic characters, Cornego and Cockadillio, as well the cameo appearances of Signor No and Medina as a French Doctor.

The two groups of characters at the centre of the play are on one hand, the ruling cabal, that is the King, his Italian Queen and their supporters, including the Italian Malateste and on the other a number of disenchanted Spanish noblemen who are in sympathy with the King's former betrothed lover, Onaelia. This later faction, led by the Duke of Medina, eventually includes the key figure of the patriotic soldier Balthazar, a man who has earned respect for his martial exploits and whose 'nobility', as celebrated in the title to the play, is a tribute earned by action rather than by birth or inheritance. He is thus differentiated from the King, whose nobility of birth is cancelled out by the dishonesty of his character.

Nevertheless, Balthazar is something of a problematic figure and in many ways an unconvincing hero for a play with ostensibly, a strong moral theme. His basic character is presented as that of an honest uncomplicated soldier; in his first appearance(2.1), he has already been slighted by the Dons, and presents an unkempt appearance and rails against the 'pied-winged butterflies' of the effete court who put appearance before patriotic duty. Nevertheless, subterfuge seems to come too readily to him as we see in 2.2 when he makes a false offer to assassinate the King to test Onaelia, again in 3.3 when he pretends to agree to murder Sebastian and Onaelia in order to placate the Queen and finally in 5.1 when he tells the King that the murder has been carried out. Scene 3.3 shows a further unedifying side of Balthazar when he bursts in on the King and stabs a servant and refuses to express remorse as the servant is a mere groom. On a different note, the character is also used to comic effect, especially in 4.2 when he acts out bawdy dialogue with Cornego. His last significant act is to dissuade the faction from attempting to assassinate the King, before being reduced to a minor role in the closing scene where he only has five short speeches and plays no significant part in the denouement. The character then, is something of a patchwork affair, playing different roles as the play progresses before being effectively jettisoned at the conclusion.

The King by contrast maintains a degree of consistency, notwithstanding his formulaic deathbed renunciation of evil. As we have seen, his Queen is Italian, but he may be associated with Italy by more reasons than his marriage. In Act 5 Scene 2, Daenia says that 'There's in his breast / Both fox and lion, and both those beasts can bite' This is an direct reference to the works of the Italian courtier Niccol˜ Machiavelli who wrote in his work on statecraft 'The Prince': 'A Prince must know how to make good use of the beasts; he should choose from among the beasts the fox and the lion; for the lion cannot defend itself from traps and the fox cannot protect itself from wolves.'

Although the book from which this extract was taken, 'The Prince', had yet to be published in English, the ideas it contained (or at least a caricature of them) had been in circulation for many years following its initial publication in Italy in 1531. These were often treated with profound suspicion by the English who saw the advocacy of the use of manipulation and deception in order to maintain power as being the idea of a disreputable foreign country. Indeed, Machiavelli was seen as a satanic figure who was known as 'Old Nick', a still-used reference to the devil, and the machiavel became a stock figure on the early modern stage, a tradition which the portrayal of the King is drawing on.

The other interesting opposition within the play is between the two claimants to the title of Queen, the current incumbent and Onaelia. There is little doubt that it is Onaelia who is the representative of virtue, her behaviour often rising above that of the 'noble' Balthazar. In Act 1 Scene 2 she makes a fearless statement in defacing the King's portrait, this being an act of treason. Despite her strong feelings however, she does not rise to Balthazar's bait when he introduces the possibility of assassinating the King; the remnants of her love for him and her concern for the stability of the realm rule this possibility out. She is not however prepared to accept her treatment without protest and, in Act 3 Scene 2, engages a poet to propagandise on her behalf. His refusal, on the grounds of self-preservation is denounced in striking terms when she accuses poets generally of being 'apt to lash / Almost to death poor wretches not worth striking / but fawn with slavish flattery on damned vices / so great men act them'. The effective conclusion of her involvement as early as the end of 3.2 impoverishes the rest of the play. The Queen's less admirable character is highlighted by the way she is prepared to condone the taking of life in order to secure her position. Her ruthless outlook is punished when she is deprived of her position and forced to return to Italy.

The final scene of the play utilises a dramatic technique that had played an important part in 'The Shoemakers' Holiday': the banquet scene. Planned by the King in an attempt to achieve reconciliation and remove the threat of Onaelia by marrying her off, it represents a means of bringing almost the entire cast on stage in order to witness the meeting out of justice. It is ironic that the King's scheme is undermined, not by his political rivals but by his allies, The Queen and Malateste, who do not believe that the marriage will provide a stable settlement and instead seek to pursue a deadlier course of action. The banquet provides the context for the unwinding of this plot as vengeance consumes itself, bring about the regime change that justice demands.

EDITORIAL PRACTICE

The text is based on the 1634 Quarto, as reproduced in Tudor Facsimile series in 1913. Spelling has been modernised, except in instances where to do so would change a word's pronunciation. Punctuation has also been modernised and has been used lightly in an attempt to reflect contemporary speech patterns. Contractions to words have been eliminated where this is possible without upsetting the verse rhythm; for example, 'baked' replaces 'bak'd' in 4.2.

Names have been retained as originally set out except that of the central character who name was spelt in the original as 'Baltazar'; Balthazar is the modern Anglicised version of the same name. The cast list has been newly compiled from the text of the play, rather than by reference to the one appearing in the Quarto.

All lines have been left justified, including those cases where characters share a line of verse. The speeches of Balthazar in the early part of 2.1 and again in 4.1 appear as verse in the Quarto but have been rendered as prose in this edition. This appears to makes more sense of the speech patterns and has the additional effect of making Balthazar and Cornego, the two non-aristocratic figures, the consistent prose speakers throughout the play.

Endnotes have been provided only to explicate words or terms of unusual obscurity. Numeric references to such notes are enclosed within angled brackets.

Stage directions may be identified as being a line of text preceded by a blank line, rather than by a character's name. These have been added to occasionally to ensure that all essential movements apparent from the text are set out. Where significant additions have been made, these are enclosed within square brackets. Scene divisions within acts have been deduced from the movements of characters.

DRAMATIS PERSONAE
King of Spain
Cardinal, advisor to the King
Count Malateste of Florence, confidant of the Queen

Roderigo, Don of Spain, supporter of the King
Valasco, Don of Spain, supporter of the King
Lopez, Don of Spain, supporter of the King
Duke of Medina, leader of the Faction
Marquis Daenia, member of the Faction
Alba, Don of Spain, member of the Faction
Carlo, Don of Spain, member of the Faction
Alanzo, Captain of the Guard, member of the Faction
Sebastian, illegitimate son of the King
Balthazar, a Spanish soldier
Cornego, servant to Onaelia
Cockadillio, a courtier
Signor No
A Poet

Queen of Spain, Paulina, daughter of Duke of Florence
Onaelia, niece to the Duke of Medina, mother of Sebastian
Juanna, maid to Onaelia
Ladies in waiting

Attendants, guards

THE PRINTER TO THE READER

Understanding reader, I present this to your view, which has received applause in action. The poet might conceive a complete satisfaction upon the stage's approbation; but the printer rests not there, knowing that that which was acted and approved upon the stage, might be no less acceptable in print. It is now communicated to you, whose leisure and knowledge admits of reading and reason. Your judgement now this Posthumous assures himself will well attest his predecessor's endeavours to give content to men of the ablest quality, such as intelligent readers are here conceived to be. I could have troubled you with a longer epistle, but I fear to stay you from the book, which affords better words and matter than I can. So the work modestly depending in the scale of your judgement, the printer for his part craves your pardon, hoping by his promptness to do you greater service, as convenience shall enable him to give you more or better testimony of his entireness towards you.

N.V.

ACT THE FIRST

SCENE I

Enter in magnificent state to the sound of loud music, the KING and QUEEN, as from church, attended by the CARDINAL, COUNT MALATESTE, MARQUIS DAENIA, RODERIGO, VALASCIO, ALBA, CARLO, and ladies-in waiting. The KING and QUEEN with courtly compliments salute and part. She exits with one half attending her. KING, CARDINAL and the other half stay, the KING seeming angry and desirous to be rid of them. KING, CARDINAL, DAENIA and others remain.

KING
Give us what no man here is master of:
Breath. Leave us pray, my father Cardinal
Can by the physic of philosophy
Set all again in order. Leave us pray.

[Exeunt. KING and CARDINAL remain.

CARDINAL
How is it with you, sir?

KING
As with a ship
Now beat with storms, now safe.
The storms are vanished
And having you my Pilot, I not only
See shore, but harbour; I to you will open
The book of a black sin, deep printed in me.
Oh father, my disease lies in my soul.

CARDINAL
The old wound sir?

KING
Yes that, it festers inwards.
For though I have a beauty to my bed
That even creation envies at, as wanting
Stuff to make such another, yet on her pillow
I lie by her, but an adulterer,
And she as an adulteress. She is my queen
And wife, yet but my strumpet though the church
Set on the seal of marriage. Good Onaelia,
Niece to our Lord High Constable of Spain
Was precontracted mine.

CARDINAL
Yet when I stung
Your conscience with remembrance of the act
Your ears were deaf to counsel.

KING
I confess it.

CARDINAL
Now to untie the knot with your new Queen

Would shake your crown half from your head.

KING
Even Troy, though she has wept her eyes out,
Would find tears to wail my kingdom's ruins.

CARDINAL
What will you do then?

KING
She has that contract written, sealed by you,
And other churchmen witnesses unto it.
A kingdom should be given for that paper.

CARDINAL
I would not, for what lies beneath the moon,
Be made a wicked engine to break in pieces
That holy contract.

KING
'Tis my soul's aim
To tie it upon a faster knot.

CARDINAL
I do not see
How you can with safe conscience get it from her.

KING
Oh I know
I wrestle with a lioness. To imprison her
And force her to it, I dare not. Death! What King
Did ever say 'I dare not'? I must have it;
A bastard have I by her, and that cock
Will have, I fear, sharp spurs, if he crow after
Him that trod for him. Something must be done
Both to the hen and the chicken. Haste you therefore
To sad Onaelia, tell her I'm resolved
To give my new hawk bells, and let her fly.
My Queen, I'm weary of, and her will marry.
To this, our text, add you what gloss you please;
The secret drifts of kings are depthless seas.

Exeunt

SCENE II

A table set out covered with black. Two waxen tapers. The King's [defaced] picture at one end and a crucifix at the other. Onaelia [dressed in black] walking discontentedly weeping to the crucifix.

A Song.

QUESTION
Oh sorrow, sorrow, say where do'st thou dwell?

ANSWER
In the lowest room of hell.

QUESTION
Art thou born of human race?

ANSWER
No, no. I have a fury's face.

QUESTION
Art thou in city, town or court?

ANSWER
I to every place resort.

QUESTION
O why into the world is sorrow sent?

ANSWER
Men afflicted best repent.

QUESTION
What dost thou feed on?

ANSWER
Broken sleep.

QUESTION
What takest thou take pleasure in?

ANSWER
To weep,
To sigh, to sob, to pine, to groan,
To wring my hands, to sit alone.

QUESTION
Oh when, oh when, shall sorrow quiet have?

ANSWER
Never, never, never, never,

Never till she finds a grave.

Enter CORNEGO.

CORNEGO
No lesson Madam but Lacrymae's?
If you had buried nine husbands, so much water as you might squeeze out of an onion had been tears enough to cast away upon fellows that cannot thank you. Come, be jovial.

ONAELIA
Sorrow becomes me best.

CORNEGO
A suit of laugh and lie down would wear better.

ONAELIA
What should I do to be merry, Cornego?

CORNGO
Be not sad.

ONELIA
But what's the best mirth in the world?

CORNEGO
Marry this, to see much, say little, do little, get little, spend little and want nothing.

ONELIA
Oh, but there is a mirth beyond all these;
This picture has so vexed me, I'm half mad,
To spite it therefore, I'll sing any song
Thyself shall tune. Say then, what mirth is best?

CORNEGO
Why then Madam, what I knock out now is the very marrowbone of mirth and this it is.

ONELIA
Say on.

CORNEGO
The best mirth for a lawyer is to have fools to his clients; for citizens to have noblemen pay for their debts; for tailors to have store of satin brought in, for then how little soever their houses are, they will be sure to have large yards. The best mirth for bawds is to have fresh handsome whores, and for whores to have rich gulls come aboard their pinnaces, for then they are sure to build galleasses.

ONELIA
These to such souls are mirth, but to mine, none.
Away.

Exit CORNEGO, Enter CARDINAL.

CARDINAL
Peace to you, Lady.

ONELIA
I will not sin so much as to hope for peace
And 'tis a mock ill suits your gravity.

CARDINAL
I come to knit the nerves of your lost strength,
To build your ruins up, to set you free
From this your voluntary banishment,
And give new being to your murdered fame.

ONELIA
What Aesculapius can do this?

CARDINAL
'Tis from the King I come.

ONELIA
A name I hate.
Oh, I am deaf now to your embassy.

CARDINAL
Hear what I speak.

ONELIA
Your language breathed from him
Is death's sad doom upon a wretch condemned.

CARDINAL
Is it such poison?

ONELIA
Yes, and were you crystal,
What the King fills you with would make you break.
You should my Lord, be like these robes you wear,
Pure as the dye, and like that reverend shape
Nurse thoughts as full of honour, zeal and purity.
You should be the court-dial, and direct
The King with constant motion, be ever beating,
Like to clock-hammers, on his iron heart
To make it sound clear and to feel remorse.
You should unlock his soul, wake his dead conscience
Which, like a drowsy sentinel, gives leave

For sin's vast armies to beleaguer him.
His ruins will be asked for at your hands.

CARDINAL
I have raised up a scaffolding to save
Both him and you from falling. Do but hear me.

ONAELIA
Be dumb for ever.

CARDINAL
Let your fears thus die:
By all the sacred relics of the church
And by my holy orders, what I minister
Is even the spirit of health.

ONAELIA
I'll drink it down into my soul at once.

CARDINAL
You shall.

ONAELIA
But swear.

CARDINAL
What conjurations can more bind my oath?

ONAELIA
But did you swear in earnest?

CARDINAL
Come, you trifle.

ONAELIA
No marvel, for my hopes have been so drowned
I still despair, say on.

CARDINAL
The King repents.

ONAELIA
Pray, that again my Lord.

CARDINAL
The King repents.

ONAELIA

His wrongs to me?

CARDINAL
His wrongs to you. The sense of sin
Has pierced his soul.

ONAELIA
Blessed penitence!

CARDINAL
Has turned his eyes into his leprous bosom
And like a king vows execution
On all his traitorous passions.

ONAELIA
God-like justice!

CARDINAL
Intends in person presently to beg
Forgiveness for his acts from heaven and you.

ONAELIA
Heaven pardon him. I shall.

CARDINAL
Will marry you.

ONAELIA
Umh! Marry me? Will he turn bigamist?
When? When?

CARDINAL
Before the morrow sun hath rode
Half his day's journey, will send home his Queen
As one that stains his bed, and can produce
Nothing but bastard issue to his crown.
Why, how now? Lost in wonder and amazement?

ONAELIA
I am so stored with joy that I can now
Strongly wear out more years of misery
Than I have lived.

Enter KING.

CARDINAL
You need not: here is the King.

KING
Leave us.

Exit CARDINAL.

ONAELIA
With pardon sir, I will prevent you
And charge upon you first.

KING
'Tis granted, do.
But stay, what mean these emblems of distress?
My picture so defaced, opposed against
A holy cross! Room hung in black, and you
Dressed like chief mourner at a funeral?

ONAELIA
Look back upon your guilt, dear Sir, and then
The cause that now seems strange explains itself.
This and the image of my living wrongs
Is still confronted by me to beget
Grief like my shame, whose length may outlive time.
This cross, the object of my wounded soul
To which I pray to keep me from despair;
That ever as the sight of one throws up
Mountains of sorrow on my accursed head.
Turning to that, mercy may check despair
And bind my hands from wilful violence.

KING
But who has played the tyrant with me thus,
And with such dangerous spite abused my picture?

ONAELIA
The guilt of that lays claim sir, to yourself
For being, by you, ransacked of all my fame,
Robbed of mine honour and dear chastity,
Made, by your act, the shame of all my house,
The hate of good men and the scorn of bad,
The song of broom-men and the murdering vulgar,
And left alone to bear up all these ills
By you begun, my breast was filled with fire
And wrapped in just disdain, and like a woman
On that dumb picture wreaked I my passions.

KING
And wished it had been I.

ONAELIA
Pardon me Sir,
My wrongs were great, and my revenge swelled high.

KING
I will descend and cease to be a King,
To leave my judging part, freely confessing
Thou canst not give thy wrongs too ill a name.
And here to make thy apprehension full,
And seat thy reason in a sound belief
I vow tomorrow, ere the rising sun
Begins his journey, with all ceremonies
Due to the Church, to seal our nuptials,
To prive thy son with full consent of state,
Spain's heir apparent, born in wedlock's vows.

ONAELIA
And will you swear to this?

KING
By this I swear.

[Takes up Bible.]

ONAELIA
Oh, you have sworn false oaths upon that book!

KING
Why then, by this.

[Takes up crucifix.]

ONAELIA
Take heed you print it deeply:
How for your concubine, bride I cannot say,
She stains your bed with black adultery,
And though her fame masks in a fairer shape
Thanmine to the world's eye, yet King, you know
Mine honour is less strumpeted than hers,
However butchered in opinion.

KING
This way for her, the contract which thou hast,
By best advice of all our Cardinals,
Today shall be enlarged till it be made
Past all dissolving. Then to our council table
Shall she be called, that read aloud, she told
The church commands her quick return for Florence

With such a dower as Spain received with her,
And that they will not hazard heaven's dire curse
To yield to a match unlawful, which shall taint
The issue of the King with bastardy.
This done, in state majestic come you forth,
Our new crowned Queen in sight of all our peers.
Are you resolved?

OMAELIA
To doubt of this were treason
Because the King has sworn it.

KING
And will keep it.
Deliver up the contract then, that I
May make this day end with thy misery.

ONAELIA
Here as the dearest Jewel of my fame
Locked I this parchment from all viewing eyes.
This your indenture, held alone the life
Of my supposed dead honour; yet behold,
Into your hands I redeliver it.
Oh keep it Sir, as you should keep that vow,
To which, being signed by heaven, even angels bow.

[ONAELIA passes the document to the KING.

KING
'Tis in the lion's paw, and who dares snatch it?
Now to your beads and crucifix again.

ONAELIA
Defend me heaven!

KING
Pray there may come Embassadors from France
Their followers are good customers.

ONAELIA
Save me from madness!

KING
'Twill raise the price, being the King's mistress.

ONAELIA
You do but counterfeit to mock my joys.

KING
Away bold strumpet!

ONAELIA
Are there eyes in heaven to see this?

KING
Call and try, here's a whore's curse
To fall in that belief, which her sins nurse.

Exit KING, Enter CORNEGO.

CORNEGO
How now? What quarter of the moon has she cut out now? My Lord puts me into a wise office to be a mad-woman's keeper. Why, Madam!

ONAELIA
Ha! Where is the King, thou slave?

[Clutches CORNEGO.]

CORNEGO
Let go your hold, or I'll fall upon you as I am a man.

ONAELIA
Thou treacherous caitiff, where is the King?

CORNEGO
He's gone, but not so far as you are.

ONAELIA
Crack all in sunder, oh you battlements,
And grind me into powder

CORNEGO
What powder? Come, what powder? When did you ever see a woman grinded into powder? I am sure some of your sex powder men, and pepper them too.

ONAELIA
Is there a vengeance yet lacking to my ruin?
Let it fall, now let it fall upon me!

CORNEGO
No, there has been too much fallen upon you already.

ONAELIA
Thou villain, leave thy hold, I'll follow him
Like a raised ghost, I'll haunt him, break his sleep,

Fright him as he is embracing his new leman,
Til want of rest bids him run mad and die,
For making oaths bawds to his perjury.

CORNEGO
Pray be more seasoned, if he make any bawds, he did ill, for there is enough of that fly-blown flesh already.

ONAELIA
I'm left quite naked now; all gone, all, all.

CORNEGO
No Madam, not all, for you cannot be rid of me.
Here comes your Uncle.

Enter MEDINA.

ONAELIA
Attired in robes of vengeance, are you uncle?

MEDINA
More horrors yet?

ONAELIA
'Twas never full till now,
And in this torrent all my hopes lie drowned.

MEDINA
Instruct me in the cause.

ONAELIA
The King, the contract!

Exit ONAELIA.

CORNEGO
That's cud enough for you to chew upon.

Exit CORNEGO.

MEDINA
What's this? A riddle. How? The King, the contract.
The mischief I divine which proving true,
Shall kindle fires in Spain to melt his crown
Even from his head. Here's the decree of fate:
A black deed must a black deed expiate.

Exit MEDINA.

ACT THE SECOND

SCENE I

Enter BALTHAZAR, having been slighted by the DONS.

BALTHAZAR
Thou god of good apparel, what strange fellows are bound to do thee honour. Mercer's books show men's devotions to thee. Heaven cannot hold a saint so stately. Do not my dons know me because I'm poor in clothes? Stood my beaten tailor plaiting my rich hose, my silk stocking man drawing upon my Lordship's courtly calf pairs of imbroidered things, whose golden clocks strike deeper to the faithful shop-keeper's heart, than into mine to pay him. Had my barber perfumed my lousy thatch here and poked out me tusks more stiff than are a cats muschatoes, these pied-winged butterflies had known me then. Another fly-boat!Save thee illustrious Don.

Enter DON RODRIGO.

Sir, is the King at leisure to speak Spanish with a poor Soldier?

RODRIGO
No

BALTHAZAR
No, Sirah, you, no! You Don with the ochre face, I wish to have thee but on a breach, stifling with smoke and fire. And for thy no, but whiffing gunpowder out of an iron pipe, I would but ask thee if thou would'st on, and if thou did'st cry no, thou should'st read Canon Law. I'd make thee roar, and wear cut-beaten-satin. I would pay thee though thou payest not thy mercer. Mere Spanish jennets!

Enter COCKADILLIO.

Signor, is the King at leisure?

COCKADILLO
To do what?

BALTHAZAR
To hear a soldier speak.

COCKADILLO
I am no ear picker
To sound his hearing that way.

BALTHAZAR
Are you of court sir?

COCKADILLO
Yes, the King's barber.

BALTHAZAR
That's his ear picker. Your name, I pray.

COCKADILLO
Don Cockadillio
If, soldier, thou hast suits to beg at court,
I shall descend so low as to betray
Thy paper to the hand Royal.

BALTHAZAR
I beg, you whorson muscod! My petition is written on my bosom in red wounds.

COCKADILLO
I am no barber-surgeon.

Exit COCKADILLIO.

BALTHAZAR
You yellowhammer, why, shaver: that such poor things as these, only made up of tailor's shreds and merchant's silken rags and 'pothecary drugs to lend their breath sophisticated smells, when their rank guts stink worse than cowards in the heat of battle. Such whaleboned-doublet rascals, that owe more to laundresses and seamsters for laced linen than all their race from their great grand-father to this their reign, in clothes were ever worth. These excrements of silk worms! Oh that such flies do buzz about the beams of Majesty, like earwigs tickling a King's yielding ear with that court-organ, flattery, when a soldier must not come near the court gates twenty score, but stand for want of clothes, though he win towns, amongst the almsbasket-men! His best reward being scorned to be a fellow to the blackguard. Why should a soldier, being the world's right arm, be cut thus by the left, a courtier? Is the world all ruff and feather and nothing else? Shall I never see a tailor give his coat with a difference from a gentleman?

Enter KING, ALANZO, CARLO, COCKADILLIO.

KING
My Balthazar!
Let us make haste to meet thee. How art thou altered?
Do you not know him?

ALANZO
Yes Sir, the brave soldier
Employed against the Moors

KING
Half turned Moor!
I'll honour thee, reach him a chair, that table
And now, Aeneas-like, let thine own trumpet
Sound forth thy battle with those slavish Moors.

BALTHAZAR
My music is a Cannon, a pitched field my stage, Furies the actors, blood and vengeance the scene, death the story, a sword imbrued with blood, the pen that writes, and the poet a terrible buskined tragical fellow, with a wreath about his head of burning match instead of bays.

KING
On to the battle.

BALTHAZAR
'Tis here without bloodshed. This our main battalia, that the van, this the vaw, these the wings, here we fight, there they fly, here they insconce, and here our sconces lay seventeen moons on the cold earth.

KING
This satisfies my eye, but now my ear
Must have his music too. Describe the battle.

BALTHAZAR
The battle? Am I come from doing to talking? The hardest part for a soldier to play is to prate well. Our tongues are fifes, drums, petronels, muskets, culverin and cannon. These are our roarers, the clocks which we go by are our hands. Thus we reckon ten, our swords strike eleven and when steel targets of proof clatter one against another, then 'tis noon that's the height and the heat of the day of battle.

KING
So.

BALTHAZAR
To that heat we came, our drums beat, pikes were shaken and shivered, swords and targets clashed and clattered, muskets rattled cannons roared, men died groaning, brave laced jerkings and feathers looked pale, tottered rascals fought pell mell. Here fell a wing, there heads were tossed like footballs, legs and arms quarrelled in the air and yet lay quietly on the earth. Horses trampled upon heaps of carcasses, troops of carbines tumbled wounded from their horses, we besiege Moors and famine us, mutinies bluster and are calm. I vowed not to doff mine armour though my flesh were frozen to it and turn into iron, nor to cut head nor beard till they yielded. My hairs and oath are of one length for, with Caesar, thus write I mine own story: veni, vidi, vici.

KING
A pitched field, quickly fought. Our hand is thine,
And because thou shalt not murmur that thy blood
Was lavished forth for an ungrateful man,
Demand what we can give thee and 'tis thine.

BALTHAZAR
Only your love.

KING
'Tis thine, rise soldier's best accord
When wounds of wrong are healed up by the sword.

ONAELIA knocks loudly at the door.

ONAELIA
Let me come in, I'll kill the treacherous King,
The murderer of mine honour, let me come in.

KING
What woman's voice is that?

ALL
Medina's niece.

KING
Bar out that fiend.

ONAELIA
I'll tear him with my nails,
Let me come in, let me come in, help, help me.

KING
Keep her from following me. A guard.

ALANZO
They are ready, sir.

KING
Let a quick summons call our Lords together,
This disease kills me.

BALTHAZAR
Sir, I would be private with you.

KING
Forebear us, but see the doors are well guarded.

[Exeunt. KING and BALTHAZAR remain.

BALTHAZAR
Will you, Sir, promise to give me freedom of speech?

KING
Yes, I will, take it, speak any thing, 'tis pardoned.

BALTHAZAR
You are a whoremaster. Do you send me to win towns for you abroad and you lose a kingdom at home?

KING

What kingdom?

BALTHAZAR
The fairest in the world, the kingdom of your fame, your honour.

KING
Wherein?

BALTHAZAR
I'll be plain with you. Much mischief is done by the mouth of a cannon, but the fire begins at a little touch-hole. You heard what nightingale sung to you even now.

KING
Ha, ha, ha!

BALTHAZAR
Angels erred but once and fell, but you Sir, spit in heaven's face every minute and laugh at it. Laugh still, follow your courses, do. Let your vices run like your kennels of hounds, yelping after you till they pluck down the fairest head in the herd, everlasting bliss.

KING
Any more?

BALTHAZAR
Take sin as the English snuff tobacco, and scornfully blow the smoke in the eyes of heaven, the vapour flies up in clouds of bravery. But when 'tis out, the coal is black, your conscience, and the pipe stinks. A sea of rosewater cannot sweeten your corrupted bosom.

KING
Nay, spit thy venom.

BALTHAZAR
'Tis Aqua Coelestis, no venom. For when you shall clasp up these two books, never to be opened again, when by letting fall that anchor which can never more be weighed up, your mortal navigation ends. Then there's no playing at spurn-point with thunderbolts. A vintner then for unconscionable reckoning or a tailor for unmeasurable items shall not answer in half that fear you must.

KING
No more.

BALTHAZAR
I will follow truth at the heels, though her foot beat my gums in pieces.

KING
The barber that draws out a lion's tooth
Curseth his trade; and so shalt thou.

BALTHAZAR

I care not.

KING
Because you have beaten a few base-born moors,
Me think'st thou to chastise? What is past I pardon,
Because I made the key to unlock thy railing;
But if thou dar'st once more be so untuned
I'll sent thee to the galleys. Who are without there,
How now?

Enter GUARDS and ATTENDANTS drawn.

ALL
In danger, Sir?

KING
Yes, yes, I am, but 'tis no point of weapon
Can rescue me. Go presently and summon
All our chief Grandees, Cardinals, and Lords
Of Spain to meet in Council instantly.
We called you forth to execute a business
Of another strain - but 'tis no matter now.
Thou diest when next thou furrowest up our brow.

BALTHAZAR
So, die!

Exit BALTHAZAR, enter CARDINAL, RODRIGO, ALBA, DAENIA, VALASCO.

KING
I find my sceptre shaken by enchantments
Charactered in this parchment, which to unloose,
I'll practice only counter-charms of fire,
And blow the spells of lightening into smoke:
Fetch burning tapers.

[Exit ATTENDANT who returns with light.

CARDINAL
Give me audience, Sir.
My apprehension opens me a way
To a close fatal mischief, worse than this
You strive to murder. Oh, this act of yours
Alone shall give your dangers life, which else
Can never grow to height. Do, Sir, but read
A book here closed up, which too late you opened,
Now blotted by you with foul marginal notes.

KING
Art frantic?

CARDINAL
You are so, Sir.

KING
If I be,
Then here's my first mad fit.

CARDINAL
For honour's sake,
For love you bear to conscience -

KING
Reach the flames:
Grandees and Lords of Spain be witness all
What here I cancel. Read, do you know this bond?

ALL
Our hands are to it.

DAENIA
'Tis your confirmed contract
With my sad kinswoman: but wherefore Sir,
Now is your rage on fire, in such a presence
To have it mourn in ashes?

KING
Marquis Daenia
We'll lend that tongue, when this no more can speak.

CARDINAL
Dear Sir!

KING
I am deaf,
Played the full concert of the spheres unto me
Upon their loudest strings - so burn that witch
Who would dry up the tree of all Spain's glories,
But that I purge her sorceries by fire.

[Burns contract.]

Troy lies in cinders. Let your Oracles
Now laugh at me if I have been deceived
By their ridiculous riddles. Why, good father,
Now you may freely chide, why was your zeal

Ready to burst in showers to quench our fury?

CARDINAL
Fury indeed, you give it proper name.
What have you done? Closed up a festering wound
Which rots the heart. Like a bad surgeon,
Labouring to pluck out from your eye a mote,
You thrust the eye clean out.

KING
Th'art mad ex tempore:
What eye? Which is that wound?

CARDINAL
That scroll, which now
You make the black indenture of your lust
Although eat up in flames, is printed here,
In me, in him, in these, in all that saw it,
In all that ever did but hear 'twas yours.
The scold of the whole world, fame, will anon
Rail with her thousand tongues at this poor shift
Which gives your sin a flame greater than that
You lend the paper. You to quench a wild fire,
Cast Oil upon it.

KING
Oil to blood shall turn,
I'll lose a limb before the heart shall mourn.

Exeunt, DAENIA and ALBA remain.

DAENIA
He's mad with rage or joy.

ALBA
With both; with rage
To see his follies checked, with fruitless joy
Because he hopes his contract is cut off,
Which divine justice more exemplifies.

Enter MEDINA.

MEDINA
Where's the King?

DAENIA
Wrapped up in clouds of lightning.

MEDINA
What has he done? Saw you the contract torn?
As I did here a minion swear he threatened.

ALBA
He tore it not, but burned it.

MEDINA
Openly!

DAENIA
And heaven with us to witness.

MEDINA
Well, that fire
Will prove a catching flame to burn his kingdom.

ALBA
Meet and consult.

MEDINA
No more, trust not the air
With our projections, let us all revenge
Wrongs done to our most noble kinswoman.
Action is honours language, swords are tongues,
Which both speak best, and best do right our wrongs.

Exeunt.

ACT THE THIRD

SCENE I

Enter ONAELIA from one way, CORNEGO another.

CORNEGO
Madam, there's a bear without to speak with you

ONAELIA
A bear?

CORNEGO
It's a man all hair, and that's as bad.

ONAELIA
Who is it?

CORNEGO
'Tis one Master Captain Balthazar.

ONAELIA
I do not know that Balthazar.

CORNEGO
He desires to see you: and if you love a water-spaniel before he be shorn, see him.

ONAELIA
Let him come in.

Enter BALTHAZAR.

CORNEGO
Hist; a duck, a duck. There she is, Sir.

BALTHAZAR
A soldier's good wish bless you lady.

ONAELIA
Good wishes are most welcome Sir, to me,
So many bad ones blast me.

BALTHAZAR
Do you not know me?

ONAELIA
I scarce know myself.

BALTHAZAR
I have been at tennis Madam, with the king. I gave him fifteen and all his faults, which is much, and now I come to toss a ball with you.

ONAELIA
I am bandied too much up and down already.

CORNEGO
Yes, she has been struck under line, master soldier.

BALTHAZAR
I conceit you, dare you trust yourself alone with me?

ONAELIA
I have been laden with such weights of wrong
That heavier cannot press me. Hence Cornego.

CORNEGO
Hence Cornego? Stay Captain? When man and woman are put together,
Some egg of villainy is sure to be sat upon.

Exit CORNEGO.

BALTHAZAR
What would you say to him should kill this man that hath you so dishonoured?

ONAELIA
Oh, I would Crown him
With thanks, praise, gold and tender of my life.

BALTHAZAR
Shall I be that German fencer, and beat all the knocking boys before me? Shall I kill him?

ONAELIA
There's music in the tongue that dares but speak it.

BALTHAZAR
That fiddle then is in me, this arm can do it, by poniard, poison or pistol: but shall I do it indeed?

ONAELIA
One step to human bliss is sweet revenge.

BALTHAZAR
Stay. What made you love him?

ONAELIA
His most goodly shape
Married to royal virtues of his mind.

BALTHAZAR
Yet now you would divorce all that goodness; and why? For a little lechery of revenge? It's a lie. The burr that sticks in your throat is a throne. Let him out of his mess of kingdoms cut out but one, and lay Sicily, Aragon or Naples or any else upon your trencher, and you will praise bastard for the sweetest wine in the world, and call for another quart of it. 'Tis not because the man has left you, but because you are not the woman you would be that mads you. A she-cuckold is an untameable monster.

ONAELIA
Monster of men thou are, thou bloody villain,
Traitor to him who never injured thee.
Dost thou profess arms, and art bound in honour
To stand up like a brazen wall to guard
Thy king and country, and would'st thou ruin both?

BALTHAZAR
You spur me on to it.

ONAELIA
True;
Worse am I then the horridest fiend in hell
To murder him who I once loved too well:
For thou I could run mad, and tear my hair,
And kill that godless man that turned me vile,
Though I am cheated by a purjurious Prince
Who has done wickedness, at which even heaven
Shakes when the sun beholds it, O yet I'd rather
Ten thousand poisoned poniards stab my breast
Than one should touch his. Bloody slave! I'll play
Myself the hangman, and will butcher thee
If thou but prickest his finger.

BALTHAZAR
Sayest thou me so! Give me thy goll, thou are a noble girl. I did play the Devil's part, and roar in a feigned voice, but I am the honestest Devil that ever spat fire. I would not drink that infernal draft of a King's blood, to go reeling to damnation, for the weight of the world in diamonds.

ONAELIA
Art thou not counterfeit?

BALTHAZAR
Now by my scars I am not.

ONAELIA
I'll call thee honest soldier then, and woo thee
To be an often visitant.

BALTHAZAR
Your servant,
Yet must I be a stone upon a hill,
For thou I do no good, I'll not lie still.

Exeunt.

ACT THE THIRD

SCENE I

Enter MALATESTE and the QUEEN.

MALATESTE
When first you came from Florence, would the world
Had with a universal dire eclipse

Been overwhelmed, no more to gaze on day,
That you to Spain had never found the way,
Here to be lost forever.

QUEEN
We from one climate
Drew suspiration. As thou then hast eyes
To read my wrongs, so be thy head an engine
To raise up ponderous mischief to the height,
And then thy hands, the executioners.
A true Italian spirit is a ball
Of wild-fire, hurting most when it seems spent.
Great ships on small rocks, beating oft are rent.
And so, let Spain by us. But Malateste,
Why from the presence did you single me
Into this gallery?

MALATESTE
To show you Madam,
The picture of yourself, but so defaced,
And mangled by proud Spaniards, it would whet
A sword to arm the poorest Florentine
In your just wrongs.

QUEEN
As how? Let's see that picture.

MALATESTE
Here 'tis then: time is not scarce four days old,
Since I, and certain Dons, sharp-witted fellows,
And of good rank, were with two Jesuits
Grave profound scholars, in deep argument
Of various propositions. At the last,
Question was moved touching your marriage
And the King's pre-contract.

QUEEN
So, and what followed?

MALATESTE
Whether it were a question moved by chance,
Or spitefully of purpose, I being there,
And your own Countryman, I cannot tell.
But when much tossing had bandied both the King
And you, as pleased those that took up the racquets.
In conclusion, the Father Jesuits,
To whose subtle music every ear there
Was tied, stood with their lives in stiff defence

Of this opinion - oh pardon me
If I must speak their language.

QUEEN
Say on.

MALATESTE
That the most Catholic king in marrying you,
Keeps you but as his whore.

QUEEN
Are we their themes?

MALATESTE
And that Medina's niece, Onaelia,
Is his true wife. Her bastard son they said
The King being dead, should claim and wear the crown,
And whatsoever children you shall bear,
To be but bastards in the highest degree,
As being begotten in adultery.

QUEEN
We will not grieve at this, but with hot vengeance
Beat down this armed mischief. Malateste!
What whirlwinds can we raise to blow this storm
Back in their faces who thus shoot at me?

MALATESTE
If I were fit to be your councillor,
Thus would I speak - feign that you are with child.
The mother of the maids, and some worn ladies
Who oft have guilty being to court great bellies,
May though it not be so, get you with child
With swearing that 'tis true.

QUEEN
Say 'tis believed,
Or that it so doth prove?

MALATESTE
The joy thereof,
Together with these earthquakes, which will shake
All Spain, if they their Prince do disinherit,
So borne, of such a Queen, being only daughter
To such a brave spirit as Duke of Florence.
All this buzzed into the King, he cannot choose
But charge that all the bells in Spain echo up
This joy to heaven, that bonfires change the night

To a high noon, with beams of sparkling flames;
And that in Churches, organs, charmed with prayers,
Speak loud for your most safe delivery.

QUEEN
What fruits grow out of these?

MALATESTE
These; you must stick,
As here and there spring weeds in banks of flowers,
Spies amongst the people, who shall lay their ears
To every mouth, and seal to you their whispering.

QUEEN
So.

MALATESTE
'Tis a plummet to sound Spanish hearts
How deeply they are yours. Besides a guesse
Is hereby made of any faction
That shall combine against you, which the King seeing,
If then he will not rouse him like a dragon
To guard his golden fleece, and rid his harlot
And her base bastard hence, either by death,
Or in some traps of state ensnare them both,
Let his own ruins crush him.

QUEEN
This goes to trial.
Be thou my magic book, which reading o'er
Their counterspells we'll break; or if the King
Will not by strong hand fix me in his Throne,
But that I must be held Spain's blazing star,
Be it an ominous charm to call up war.

SCENE II

Enter CORNEGO and ONAELIA.

CORNEGO
Here's a parcel of man's flesh has been hanging up and down all this morning to speak with you.

ONAELIA
Is't not some executioner?

CORNEGO

I see nothing about him to hang in but his garters.

ONAELIA
Sent from the King to warn me of my death:
I prithee bid him welcome.

CORNEGO
He says he is a poet.

ONAELIA
Then bid him better welcome.
Belike he's come to write my epitaph,
Some scurvy thing I'll warrant. Welcome Sir.

Enter POET.

POET
Madam, my love presents this book unto you.

ONAELIA
To me? I am not worthy of a line,
Unless at that Line hang some hook to choke me:

[ONAELIA reads book.]

To the Most Honoured Lady - Onaelia.
Fellow thou liest, I'm most dishonoured:
Thou should'st have writ to the most wronged Lady.
The title of this book is not to me,
I tear it therefore as mine honour's torn.

CORNEGO
Your verses are lamed in some of their feet, Master poet.

ONAELIA
What does it treat of?

POET
Of the solemn triumphs
Set forth at coronation of the Queen.

ONAELIA
Hissing, the poet's whirlwind, blast thy lines!
Com'st thou to mock my tortures with her triumphs?

POET
'Las Madam!

ONAELIA
When her funerals are past,
Crown thou a dedication to my joys,
And thou shalt swear each line a golden verse.
Cornego, burn this idol.

CORNGO
Your book shall come to light, Sir.

Exit CORNEGO with book.

ONAELIA
I have read legends of disastrous dames;
Will none set pen to paper for poor me?
Canst write a bitter satire? Brainless people
Do call them libels. Darest thou write a libel?

POET
I dare mix gall and poison with my ink.

ONAELIA
Do it then for me.

POET
And every line must be
A whip to draw blood.

ONAELIA
Better.

POET
And to dare
The stab from him it touches. He that writes
Such libels, as you call them, must launch wide
The sores of men's corruptions, and even search
To the quick for dead flesh, or for rotten cores:
A poet's ink can better cure some sores
Than surgeon's balsam.

ONAELIA
Undertake that cure
And crown thy verse with bays.

POET
Madam, I'll do it,
But I must have the party's character.

ONAELIA

The King.

POET
I do not love to pluck the quills,
With which I make pens, out of a lion's claw.
The King! Should I be bitter 'gainst the King,
I shall have scurvy ballads made of me,
Sung to the hanging tune. I dare not, Madam.

ONAELIA
This baseness follows your profession.
You are like common beadles, apt to lash
Almost to death poor wretches not worth striking,
But fawn with slavish flattery on damned vices
So great men act them. You clap hands at those,
Where the true poet indeed doth scorn to guild
A gaudy tomb with glory of his verse,
Which coffins stinking carrion. No, his lines
Are free as his invention. No base fear
Can shake his pen to temporise even with kings,
The blacker are their crimes, he louder sings.
Go, go, thou canst not write: 'tis but my calling
The muses help, that I may be inspired.
Canst a woman be a poet, Sir?

POET
Yes, Madam, best of all. For poesie
Is but feigning, feigning is to lie,
And women practice lying more than men.

ONAELIA
Nay, but if I should write, I would tell truth.
How might I reach a lofty strain?

POET
Thus Madam:
Books, music, wine, brave company and good cheer
Make poets to soar high and sing most clear.

ONAELIA
Are they born poets?

POET
Yes.

ONAELIA
Die they?

POET
Oh, never die.

ONAELIA
My misery is then a poet sure,
For time has given it an eternity.
What sort of poets are there?

POET
Two sorts lady:
The great poets and the small poets.

ONAELIA
Great and small!
Which do you call the great? The fat ones?

POET
No:
But such as have great heads, which emptied forth,
Fill all the world with wonder at their lines;
Fellows which swell big with the wind of praise.
The small ones are but shrimps of poesie.

ONAELIA
Which in the kingdom now is the best poet?

POET
Emulation.

ONAELIA
Which the next?

POET
Necessity.

ONAELIA
And which the worst?

POET
Self-love.

ONAELIA
Say I turn poet, what should I get?

POET
Opinion.

ONAELIA

Alas, I have got too much of that already,
Opinion is my evidence, judge and jury.
Mine own guilt and opinion now condemn me.
I'll therefore be no poet, no nor make
Ten muses of your nine. I'll swear for this;
Verses, though freely born, like slaves are sold,
I crown thy lines with bays, thy love with gold:
So fare thou well.

POET
Our pen shall honour thee.

Exit POET, enter CORNEGO.

CORNEGO
The poet's book Madam, has got the inflammation of the liver, it died of a burning fever.

ONAELIA
What shall I do, Cornego? For this poet
Has filled me with a fury. I could write
Strange satires now against adulterers,
And marriage-breakers.

CORNEGO
I believe you Madam - but here comes your uncle.

Enter MEDINA, ALANZO, CARLO, ALBA, SEBASTIAN, DAENIA.

MEDINA
Where's our niece?
Turn your brains round, and recollect your spirits,
And see your noble friends and kinsmen ready
To pay revenge his due.

ONAELIA
That word revenge,
Startles my sleepy soul, now thoroughly wakened
By the fresh object of my hapless child
Whose wrongs reach beyond mine.

SEBASTIAN
How doth my sweet mother?

ONAELIA
How doth my prettiest boy?

ALANZO
Wrongs, like great whirlwinds,

Shake highest battlements. Few for heaven would care,
Should they be ever happy. They are half gods
Who both in good days, and good fortune share.

ONAELIA
I have no part in either.

CARLO
You shall in both,
Can swords but cut the way.

ONAELIA
I care not much, so you but gently strike him,
And that my child escape the lightening.

MEDINA
For that our nerves are knit; is there not here
A promising face of manly princely virtues,
And shall so sweet a plant be rooted out
By him that ought to fix it fast in the ground?
Sebastian, what will you do to him
That hurts your mother?

SEBASTIAN
The King my father shall kill him I trow.

DAENIA
But sweet cousin, the King loves not your mother.

SEBASTIAN
I'll make him love her when I am a King.

MEDINA
La you, there's in him a king's heart already.
As therefore we before together vowed,
Lay all your warlike hands upon my sword,
And swear.

SEBASTIAN
Will you swear to kill me, Uncle?

MEDINA
Oh not for twenty worlds.

SEBASTIAN
Nay then draw and spare not, for I love fighting.

MEDINA

Stand in the midst, sweet coz, we are your guard.
These hammers shall for thee beat out a crown
If all hit right. Swear therefore, noble friends,
By your high bloods, by true nobility,
By what you owe religion, owe to your country,
Owe to the raising your posterity,
By love you bear to virtue, and to arms,
The shield of innocence, swear not to sheath
Your swords, when once drawn forth.

ONAELIA
Oh not to kill him
For twenty thousand worlds.

MEDINA
Will you be quiet?
Your swords when once drawn forth, till they have forced
Yon godless, perjurous, perfidious man...

ONAELIA
Pray rail not at him so.

MEDINA
Art mad? You're idle
Till they have forced him
To cancel his late lawless bond he sealed
At the high altar to his Florentine strumpet,
And in his bed lay this his troth-plight wife.

ONAELIA
I, I that's well. Pray swear.

ALL
To this we swear.

SEBASTIAN
Uncle, I swear too.

MEDINA
Our forces let's unite, be bold and secret,
And lion-like with open eyes let's sleep,
Streams smooth and slowly running are most deep.

Exeunt.

SCENE III

Enter KING, QUEEN, MALATESTE, VALASCO, LOPEZ, RODERIGO and GUARDS.

KING
The presence door be guarded, let none enter
On forfeit of your lives, without our knowledge.
Oh you are false physicians all unto me,
You bring me poison, but no antidotes.

QUEEN
Yourself that poison brews.

KING
Prithee, no more.

QUEEN
I will, I must speak more.

KING
Thunder aloud.

QUEEN
My child, yet newly quickened in my womb,
Is blasted with the fires of bastardy.

KING
Who! Who dares once but think so in his dream?

MALATESTE
Medina's faction preached it openly.

KING
Be cursed he and his faction. Oh how I labour
For these preventions! But so cross is fate
My ills are ne'r hid from me, but their cures.
What's to be done?

QUEEN
That which being left undone,
Your life lies at the stake. Let them be breathless
Both brat and mother.

KING
Ha!

MALATESTE
She plays true music Sir.
The mischiefs you are drenched in are so full,

You need not fear to add to them. Since now
No way is left to guard thy rest secure,
But by a means like this.

LOPEZ
All Spain rings forth
Medina's name, and his confederates.

RODRIGO
All his allies and friends rush into troops
Like raging torrents.

VALESCO
And loud trumpet forth
Your perjuries. Seducing the wild people,
And with rebellious faces threatening all.

KING
I shall be massacred in this their spleen,
Ere I have time to guard myself. I feel
The fire already falling. Where's our guard?

MALATESTE
Planted at guarded gate, with a strict charge
That none shall enter but by your command.

KING
Let them be doubled. I am full of thoughts,
A thousand wheels toss my incertain fears,
There is a storm in my hot boiling brains,
Which rises without wind. A horrid one.
What clamour's that?

QUEEN
Some treason. Guard the King.

Enter BALTHAZAR drawn, he strikes one of the guards who falls.

BALTHAZAR
Not in?

MALATESTE
One of the guards is slain, keep off the murderer.

BALTHAZAR
I am none, sir.

VALASCO

There's a man dropped down by thee.

KING
Thou desperate fellow, thus press in upon us!
Is murder all the story we shall read?
What King can stand, when thus his subjects bleed?
What has thou done?

BALTHAZAR
No hurt.

KING
Played even the wolf,
And from a fold committed to my charge,
Stolen and devoured one of the flock.

BALTHAZAR
You have sheep enough for all that, Sir. I have killed none though.
Or if I have, mine own blood, shed in your quarrels, may beg my pardon.
My business was in haste to you.

KING
I would not have thy sin scored on my head
For all the Indian Treasury. I prithee tell me,
Suppose thou had'st our pardon, oh can that cure
Thy wounded conscience, can there my pardon help thee?
Yet having deserved well both of Spain and us,
We will not pay thy worth with loss of life,
But banish thee for ever.

BALTHAZAR
For a groom's death?

KING
No more. We banish thee our court and Kingdom.
A King that fosters men so dipped in blood,
May be called merciful, but never good.
Be gone upon thy life.

BALTHAZAR
Well, farewell.

Exit BALTHAZAR.

VALASCO
The fellow is not dead, but wounded sir.

QUEEN

After him Malateste. In our lodging
Stay that rough fellow, he's the man shall do't.
Haste or my hopes are lost.

Exit MALATESTE.

Why are you sad, sir?

KING
For thee, Paulina, swell my troubled thoughts
Like billows beaten by two warring winds.

QUEEN
Be you ruled but ruled by me, I'll make a calm
Smooth as the breast of heaven.

KING
Instruct me how.

QUEEN
You, as your fortunes tie you, are inclined
To have the blow given.

KING
Where's the instrument?

QUEEN
'Tis found in Balthazar.

KING
He's banished.

QUEEN
True
But stayed by me for this.

KING
His spirit is hot
And rugged, but so honest that his soul
Will never turn devil to do it.

QUEEN
Put it to trial.
Retire a little, hither I'll send for him,
Offer repeal and favours if he do it.
But if he deny, you have no finger in't,
And then his doom of banishment stands good.

KING
Be happy in thy workings, I obey.

Exit KING

QUEEN
Stay Lopez.

LOPEZ
Madam.

QUEEN
Step to our lodging, Lopez
And instantly bid Malateste bring
The banished Balthazar to us.

LOPEZ
I shall.

Exit LOPEZ.

QUEEN
Thrive my black plots, the mischiefs I have set
Must not so die. Ills must new ills beget.

Enter MALATESTE and BALTHAZAR.

BALTHAZAR
Now! What hot poisoned custard must I put my spoon into now?

QUEEN
None, for mine honour is now thy protection.

MALATESTE
Which, noble soldier, she will pawn for thee
But never forfeit.

BALTHAZAR
'Tis a fair gage, keep it.

QUEEN
Oh Balthazar! I am thy friend, and marked thee.
When the King sentenced thee to banishment
Fire sparkled from thine eyes of rage and grief.
Rage to be doomed so for a groom so base,
And grief to lose thy Country. Thou hast killed none,
The milk-sop is but wounded, thou are not banished.

BALTHAZAR
If I were, I lose nothing, I can make any country mine. I have a private coat for Italian Stilettos, I can be treacherous with the Walloon, drunk with the Dutch, a chimney-sweeper with the Irish, a gentleman with the Welsh and true arrant thief with the English. What then is my country to me?

QUEEN
The King, who rap'd with fury, banished thee,
Shall give thee favours, yield but to destroy
What him distempers.

BALTHAZAR
So. And what is the dish I must dress?

QUEEN
Only the cutting off a pair of lives.

BALTHAZAR
I love no red-wine healths.

QUEEN
The King commands it, you are but executioner.

BALTHAZAR
The hang-man? An office that will hold so long as hemp lasts. Why do not you beg the office, Sir?

QUEEN
Thy victories in field never did crown thee
As this one Act shall.

BALTHAZAR
Prove but that, 'tis done.

QUEEN
Follow him close, he's yielding.

MALATESTE
Thou shalt be called thy Country's Patriot,
For quenching out a fire now newly kindling
In factious bosoms, and shalt thereby save
More Noble Spaniards lives, than thou slew Moors.

QUEEN
Art thou yet converted?

BALTHAZAR
No point.

QUEEN

Read me then:
Medina's niece, by a contract from the King,
Lays claim to all that's mine, my crown, my bed.
A son she has by him must fill the throne,
If her great faction can but work that wonder.
Now hear me...

BALTHAZAR
I do with gaping ears.

QUEEN
I swell with hopeful issue to the King.

BALTHAZAR
A brave Don call you mother.

MALATESTE
Of this danger the fear afflicts the King.

BALATAZAR
Cannot much blame him.

QUEEN
If therefore by the riddance of this Dame ...

BALTHAZAR
Riddance? Oh! The meaning on't is murder.

MALATESTE
Stab her, or so, that's all.

QUEEN
That Spain be free from frights, the King from fears,
And I, now held his infamy, be called Queen,
The treasure of the Kingdom shall lie open
To pay thy noble darings.

BALTHAZAR
Come. I'll do it, provided I hear Jove call to me, though he roars. I must have the King's hand to this warrant, else I dare not serve it upon my conscience.

QUEEN
Be firm then. Behold the King is come.

Enter KING.

BALTHAZAR
Acquaint him.

QUEEN
I found the metal hard, but with oft beating
He's now so softened, he shall take impression
From any seal you give him.

KING
Balthazar,
Come hither, listen. Whatsoe'er our Queen
Has importuned thee to touching Onaelia
Niece to the Constable, and her young son,
My voice shall second it, and sign her promise.

BALTHAZAR
Their riddance?

KING
That.

BALTHAZAR
What way? By poison?

KING
So.

BALTHAZAR
Starving? Or strangling, stabbing, smothering?

QUEEN
Good.

KING
Any way, so 'tis done.

BALTHAZAR
But I will have, Sir,
This under your own hand, that you desire it,
You plot it, set me on to't.

KING
Pen, ink and paper.

[KING writes and signs document.]

BALTHAZAR
And then as large a pardon as law and wit can engross for me.

KING

Thou shalt have my pardon.

BALTHAZAR
A word more, Sir, pray will you tell me one thing?

KING
Yes, any thing dear Balthazar.

BALTHAZAR
Suppose I have your strongest pardon, can that cure my wounded conscience? Can there your pardon help me? You not only knock the ewe on the head, but cut the innocent lamb's throat too, yet you are no butcher.

QUEEN
Is this thy promised yielding to an act
So wholesome for thy country?

KING
Chide him not.

BALTHAZAR
I would not have this sin scored on my head
For all the Indian Treasury.

KING
That song no more.
Do this and I will make thee a great man.

BALTHAZAR
Is there no farther trick in't but my blow, your purse and my pardon?

MALTATESTE
No nets upon my life to entrap thee.

BALTHAZAR
Then trust me. These knuckles work it.

KING
Farewell. Be confident and sudden.

BALTHAZAR
Yes.
Subjects may stumble, when kings walk astray.
Thine Acts shall be a new Apocrypha.

Exeunt.

ACT THE FOURTH

SCENE I

Enter MEDINA, ALBA, CARLO, and DAENIA, met by BALTHAZAR with a poniard and a pistol.

BALTHAZAR
You met a Hydra. See, if one head fails
Another with a sulphurous beak stands yawning.

MEDINA
What hath raised up this devil?

BALTHAZAR
A great man's vices, that can raise all hell. What would you call that man, who under-sail in a most goodly ship, wherein he ventures his life, fortunes, and honours, yet in a fury should hew the mast down, cast sails overboard, fire all the tacklings, and to crown this madness, should blow up all the decks, burn th'oaken ribs, and in that combat 'twix two elements leap desperately, and drown himself in the seas? What were so brave a fellow?

ALL
A brave black villain.

BALTHAZAR
That's I. All that brave black villain dwells in me, if I be that black villain. But I am not! A nobler character prints out my brow, which you may thus read, I was banished Spain for emptying a court- hogshead, but repealed so I would, ere my reeking iron was cold, promise to give it a deep crimson dye in - none hear, - stay - no, none hear.

MEDINA
Whom then?

BALTHAZAR
Basely to stab a woman, your wronged niece and her most innocent son,
Sebastian.

ALBA
The boar now foams with wetting.

DAENIA
What has blunted
Thy weapons point at these?

BALTHAZAR
My honesty. A sign at which few dwell, pure honesty! I am a vassal to Medina's house, He taught me first the A-B-C of war. E'er I was truncheon high, I had the stile on beardless Captain, writing then but

boy, and shall I now turn slave to him that fed me with Cannon- bullets and taught me, ostrich-like to digest iron and steel! No! Yet I yielded with willow-bendings to commanding breaths.

MEDINA
Of whom?

BALTHAZAR
Of King and Queen. With supple hams and an ill-boding look, I vowed to do it. Yet, lest some choke-pear of state policy should stop my throat, and spoil my drinking pipe, see, like his cloak, I hung at the King's elbow, till I had got his hand to sign my life.

[BALTHAZAR passes over the document signed by the KING.]

DAENIA
Shall we see this and sleep?

ALBA
No, whilst these wake.

MEDINA
'Tis the King's hand?

BALTHAZAR
Think you me a coiner?

MEDINA
No, no,
Thou art thy self still, noble Balthazar.
I ever knew thee honest, and the mark
Stands still upon thy forehead.

BALTHAZAR
Else flea the skin off.

MEDINA
I ever knew thee valiant, and to scorn
All acts of baseness. I have seen this man
Write in the field such stories with his sword,
That our best chieftains swore there was in him
As 'twere a new philosophy of fighting,
His deeds were so punctilious. In one battle
When death so nearly missed my ribs, he struck
Three horses stone-dead under me. This man,
Three times that day, even through the jaws of danger,
Redeemed me up and, I shall print it ever,
Stood over my body with Colossus thighs
Whilst all the thunder-bolts which war could throw,
Fell on his head. And Balthazar, thou canst not

Be now but honest still, and valiant still,
Not to kill boys and women.

BALTHAZAR
My biter here, eats no such meat.

MEDINA
Go fetch the marked-out lamb for slaughter hither,
Good fellow-soldier aid him, and stay, mark,
Give this false fire to the believing King,
That the child's sent to heaven, but that the mother
Stands rocked so strong with friends, ten thousand billows
Cannot once shake her.

BALTHAZAR
This I'll do.

MEDINA
Away.
Yet one word more. Your counsel, Noble friends.
Hark Balthazar, because nor eyes nor tongues,
Shall by loud larums, that the poor boy lives,
Question thy false report, the child shall, closely
Mantled in darkness, forthwith be conveyed
To the monastery of Saint Paul.

ALL
Good.

MEDINA
Despatch then, be quick.

BALTHAZAR
As lightning.

Exit BALTHAZAR.

ALBA
This fellow is some angel dropped from heaven
To preserve innocence.

MEDINA
He is a wheel
Of swift and turbulent motion. I have trusted him,
Yet will not hang on him too many plummets,
Lest with a headlong gyre he ruins all.
In these state consternations, when a kingdom
Stands tottering at the centre, out of suspicion

Safety grows often. Let us suspect this fellow,
And that albeit he show us the King's hand,
It may be but a trick.

DAENIA
Your Lordship hits
A poisoned nail i'th head. This waxen fellow,
By the King's hand so bribing him with gold,
Is set on screws, perhaps is made his creature,
To turn round every way.

MEDINA
Out of that fear
Will I beget truth. For myself in person
Will sound the King's breast.

CARLO
How? Yourself in person?

ALBA
That's half the prize he gapes for.

MEDINA
I'll venture it,
And come off well I warrant you, and rip up
His very entrails, cut in two his heart,
And search each corner in't, yet shall not he
Know who it is cut up the anatomy.

DAENIA
'Tis an exploit worth wonder.

CARLO
Put the worst,
Say some infernal voice should roar from hell,
The infant's cloistering up.

ALBA
'Tis not our danger,
Nor the imprisoned Prince's, for what thief
Dares by base sacrilege rob the Church of him?

CARLO
At worst none can be lost but this slight fellow!

MEDINA
All build on this as on a stable cube.
If we our footing keep, we fetch him forth,

And crown him King. If up we fly i'th air,
We for his soul's health a broad way prepare.

DAENIS
They come.

Enter Balthazar and Sebastian.

MEDINA
Thou knowest where to bestow him, Balthazar.

BALTHAZAR
Come noble boy.

ALBA
Hide him from being discovered.

BALTHAZAR
Discovered? Would there stood a troop of Moors thrusting the paws of hungry lions forth, to seize this prey, and this but in my hand, I should do something.

SEBASTIAN
Must I go with this black fellow, Uncle?

MEDINA
Yes, pretty coz, hence with him Balthazar.

BALTHAZAR
Sweet child, within few minutes I'll change thy fate
And take thee hence, but set thee at heavens gate.

[Exit BALTHAZAR and SEBASTIAN.]

MEDINA
Some keep aloof and watch this soldier

CARLO
I'll do't.

Exit CARLO.

DAENIA
What's to be done now?

MEDINA
First to plant strong guard
About the mother, then into some snare
To hunt this spotted panther, and there kill him.

DAENIA
What snares have we can hold him?

MEDINA
Be that care mine.
Dangers, like stars, in dark attempts best shine.

Exeunt.

SCENE II

Enter CORNEGO, BALTHAZAR.

CORNEGO
The Lady Onaelia dresseth the stead of her commendations in the most courtly attire that words can be clothed with, from herself to you, by me.

BALTHAZAR
So Sir, and what disease troubles her now?

CORNEGO
The King's evil. And here she hath sent something to you, wrapped up in a white sheet, you need not fear to open it, 'tis no course.

BALTHAZAR
What's here? A letter minced into five morsels? What was she doing when thou camest from her?

CORNEGO
At her prick-song.

BALTHAZAR
So me thinks, for here's nothing but sol-re-me-fa-mi. What crotchet fills her head now, canst tell?

CORNEGO
No crotchets, 'tis only the Cliff has made her mad.

BALTHAZAR
What instrument played she upon?

CORNEGO
A wind instrument, she did nothing but sigh.

BALTHAZAR
Sol, re, me, fa, mi.

CORNEGO
My wit has always a singing head, I have found out her note captain.

BALTHAZAR
The tune? Come.

CORNEGO
Sol, my soul. Re, is all rent and torn like a ragamuffin. Me, mend it good captain. Fa, fa. What's fa Captain?

BALTHAZAR
Fa, why farewell and be hanged.

CORNEGO
Mi Captain, with all my heart. Have I tickled my Lady's fiddle well?

BALTHAZAR
Oh, but you stick wants rosin to make the strings sound clearly. No, this double virginal, being cunningly touched, another matter of jack leaps up then is now in mine eye. Sol, re me fa, mi, I have it now. Solus Rex me facit miseram. Alas poor Lady, tell her no apothecary in Spain has any of that assa foetida she writes for.

CORNEGO
Assa foetida? What's that?

BALTHAZARA
A thing to be taken in a glister-pipe.

CORNEGO
Why, what ails my Lady?

BALTHAZAR
What ails she? Why when she cries out, Solus Rex me facit miseram, she says in the Hypocronicall language, that she is so miserably tormented with the wind colic that it racks her very soul.

CORNEGO
I said somewhat cut her soul in pieces.

BALTHAZAR
But go to her, and say the oven is heating.

CORNEGO
And what shall be baked in't?

BALTHAZAR
Carp pies. And besides, tell her the hole in her coat shall be mended, and tell her if the dial of good days goes true, why then bounce buckrum.

CORNEGO
The devil lies sick of the mulligrubs.

BALTHAZAR
Or the Cony is dub'd, and three sheepskins ...

CORNEGO
With the wrong side outward ...

BALTHAZAR
Shall make the fox a night-cap.

CORNEGO
So the goose talks French to the buzzard.

BALTHAZAR
But, Sir, if evil days jostle our prognostication to the wall, then say there's a fire in a whore-masters cod-piece.

CORNEGO
And a poisoned bag-pudding in Tom Thumb's belly.

BALTHAZAR
The first cut be thine. Farewell.

CORNEGO
Is this all?

BALTHAZAR
Would'st not trust an Almanac?

CORNEGO
Not a coranta neither, though it were sealed with butter, and yet I know where they both lie passing well.

Enter LOPEZ.

LOPEZ
The King sends round about the court to seek you.

BALTHAZAR
Away Otterhound.

CORNEGO
Dancing bear, I'm gone.

Exit CORNEGO. Enter KING attended.

KING
A Private room,

Exeunt, KING and BALTHAZAR remain

I'st done? Hast drawn thy two-edged sword out yet?

BALTHAZAR
No, I was striking at the two iron bars that hinder your passage, and see Sir.

Draws.

KING
What mean'st thou?

BALTHAZAR
The edge abated, feel.

KING
No, no I see it.

BALTHAZAR
As blunt as ignorance.

KING
How? Put up - so - how?

BALTHAZAR
I saw by chance hanging in Cardinal Alvarez gallery, a picture of hell.

KING
So what of that?

BALTHAZAR
There lay upon burnt straw ten thousand brave fellows all stark naked, some leaning upon crowns, some on Mitres, some on bags of gold. Glory, in another corner lay, a feather beaten in the rain. Beauty was turned into a watching candle that went out stinking. Ambition went upon a huge high pair of stilts but horribly rotten. Some in another nook were killing Kings, and some having their elbows shoved forward by Kings to murder others. I was, me thought, half in hell myself whist I stood to view this piece.

KING
Was this all?

BALTHAZAR
Was't not enough to see that a man is more healthful that eats dirty puddings, than he that feeds on a corrupted conscience?

KING

Conscience! What's that? A conjuring book ne'r opened
Without the reader's danger. 'Tis indeed
A scarecrow set i'th world to frighten weak fools.
Hast thou seen fields paved o'er with carcasses,
Now to be tender-footed, not to tread
On a boy's mangled quarters, and a woman's!

BALTHAZAR
Nay, Sir, I have searched the records of the Low-Countries, and find that by your pardon I need not care a pin for goblins, and therefore I will do it Sir. I did recoil because I was double charged.

KING
No more. Here comes a satyr with sharp horns.

Enter CARDINAL, and MEDINA like a French Doctor.

CARDINAL
Sir, here's a Frenchman charged with some strange business
Which to close ear only he'll deliver,
Or else to none.

KING
A Frenchman?

MEDINA
Oui, Monsieur.

KING
Cannot he speak the Spanish?

MEDINA
Si Signor, un Poco - Monsieur Acontez in de Corner, me come for offer to your Bon Grace mi trezhumbla service, by gar no John fidleco shall put into your near braver melody dan dis un petite pipe shall play to your great bon Grace.

KING
What is the tune you strike up, touch the string.

MEDINA
Dis - me has run up and down mine Country and learn many fine thing, and mush knavery, now more and all dis me know you'll jumbla de fine vench and fill her belly with garsoone, her name is La Madam.

KING
Onaelia.

MEDINA

She by gar. Now Monsieur dis Madam send for me to help her malady, being very naught of her corpus, her body, me know you no point loves dis vench. But royal Monsieur donne moye ten thousand French Crowns she shall kick up her tail by gar, and beshide lie dead as dog in de shannell.

KING
Speak low.

MEDINA
As de bag-pipe when de wind is puff, Gar beigh,

KING
Thou namest ten thousand Crowns, I'll treble them
Rid me of this leprosy. Thy name?

MEDINA
Monsieur Doctor Devil.

KING
Shall I a second wheel add to this mischief
To set it faster going? If one break,
T'other may keep his motion.

MEDINA
Esselent fort boone.

KING
Balthazar.
To give thy sword an edge again, this Frenchman
Shall whet thee on, that if thy pistol fail,
Or poniard, this can send the poison home.

BALTHAZAR
Brother Cain we'll shake hands.

MEDINA
In de bowl of de bloody busher. 'Tis very fine wholesome.

KING
And more to arm your resolution,
I'll tune this Churchman so, that he shall chime
In sounds harmonious, merit to that man
Whose hand has but a finger in that act.

BALTHAZAR
That music were worth hearing.

KING
Holy father,

You must give pardon to me in unlocking
A cave stuffed full with serpents, which my State
Threaten to poison, and it lies in you
To break their bed with thunder of your voice.

CARDINAL
How princely son?

KING
Suppose a universal
Hot pestilence beat her mortiferous wings
O'er all my kingdoms, am I not bound in soul,
To empty all our academies of doctors
And Aesculapian spirits to charm this plague?

CARDINAL
You are.

KING
Or had the canon made a breach
Into our rich Escurial, down to beat it
About our ears, should I stop this breach
Spare even our richest Ornaments, nay our crown,
Could it keep bullets off.

CARDINAL
No sir, you should not.

KING
This linstock gives you fire. Shall then that strumpet
And bastard breathe quick vengeance in my face,
Making my Kingdom reel, my subjects stagger
In their obedience, and yet live?

CARDINAL
How? Live!
Shed not their bloods to gain a kingdom greater
Than ten times this.

MEDINA
Pish, not matter how Red-cap and his wit run.

KING
As I am Catholic King, I'll have their hearts
Panting in these two hands.

CARDINAL
Dare you turn hangman?

Is this religion Catholic to kill
What even brute beasts abhor to do, your own!
To cut in sunder wedlock's sacred knot
Tied by heaven's fingers! To make Spain a bonfire
To quench which must a second deluge rain
In showers of blood, no water. If you do this
There is an arm armipotent that can fling you
Into a base grave, and your palaces
With lightening strike, and of their ruins make
A tomb for you, unpitied and abhorred,
Bear witness all you lamps celestial
I wash my hands of this.

KING
Rise my good angel,
Whose holy tunes beat from me that evil spirit
Which jogs mine elbow, hence thou dog of hell.

MEDINA
Bow wow.

KING
Bark out no more thou mastiff, get you all gone,
And let my soul sleep. [Aside to BALTHAZAR]
There's gold, peace, see it done.

Exit KING.

BALTHAZAR
Sirra, you salsa-perilla, rascal, toads-gut, you whorson pockey
French spawn of a butsten-bellyed spider. Do you hear Monsieur?

MEDINA
Why do you bark and snap at my Narcissus, as if I were de French dog?

BALTHAZAR
You cur of Cerberus litter,

[Strikes him]

You'll poison the honest Lady? Do but once toot into her chamber-pot, and I'll make thee look worse than a witch does upon a close stool.

CARDINAL
You shall not dare to touch him, stood he here
Single before thee.

BALTHAZAR

I'll cut the rat into anchovies.

CARDINAL
I'll make thee kiss his hand, embrace him, love him
And call him ...

Medina [reveals his true identity].

BALTHAZAR
The perfection of all Spaniards, Mars in little, the best book of the art of war printed in these times. As a French doctor, I would have given you pellets for pills, but as my noblest Lord, rip my heart out in your service.

MEDINA
Thou are the truest Clock
That e'er to time paidst tribute, honest soldier,
I lost mine own shape, and put on a French
Only to try thy truth, and the King's falsehood,
Both which I find. Now this great Spanish volume
Is opened to me, I read him o'er and o'er,
Oh what black characters are printed in him.

CARDINAL
Nothing but certain ruin threats your niece,
Without prevention. Well this plot was laid
In such disguise to sound him, they that know
How to meet dangers, are the less afraid.
Yet let me counsel you not to text down
These wrongs in red lines.

MEDINA
No, I will not, father.
Now that I have anatomised his thoughts,
I'll read a lecture on them that shall save
Many men's lives, and to the kingdom minister
Most wholesome surgery. Here's our aphorism.
These letters from us in our niece's name,
You know treat of a marriage.

CARDINAL
There's the strong anchor
To stay all in this tempest.

MEDINA
Holy sir,
With these works you the King, and so prevail
That all these mischiefs hull with flagging sail.

CARDINAL
My best in this I'll do.

MEDINA
Soldier, thy breast
I must lock better things in.

BALTHAZAR
'Tis your chest,
With three good keys to keep it from opening an honest heart, a daring hand, and a pocket which scorns money.

Exeunt.

ACT THE FIFTH

SCENE I

Enter KING, CARDINAL with letters, VALESCO and LOPEZ.

KING
Commend us to Medina, say his letters
Right pleasing are, and that, except himself
Nothing could be more welcome. Counsel him,
To blot the opinion out of factious numbers,
Only to have his ordinary train
Waiting upon him. For, to quit all fears
Upon his side of us, our very court
Shall even but dimly shine with some few Dons,
Freely to prove our longings great to peace.

CARDINAL
The Constable expects some pawn from you,
That in this fairy circle shall rise up
No fury to confound his niece nor him.

KING
A King's word is engaged.

CARDINAL
It shall be taken.

KING
Valasco, call the Captain of our Guard,
Bid him attend us instantly.

VALASCO
I shall.

Exit VALASCO.

KING
Lopez come hither. See,
Letters from Duke Medina, both in the name
Of him and all his faction, offering peace,
And our old love, his niece Onaelia
In marriage with her free and fair consent
To Cockadillio, a Don of Spain.

LOPEZ
Will you refuse this?

KING
My crown as soon. They feel their sinewy plots
Belike to shrink i'the joints. And fearing ruin,
Have found this cement out to piece up all,
Which more endangers all.

LOPEZ
How sir? Endangers!

KING
Lions may hunted be into the snare,
But if they once break loose, woe be to him
That first seized on them. A poor prisoner scorns
To kiss his jailer. And shall a king be choked
With sweet-meats by false traitors! No, I will fawn
On them as they stroke me, till they are fast
But in this paw. And then...

LOPEZ
A brave revenge!
The Captain of your Guard.

Enter ALANZO, the Captain.

KING
Upon thy life
Double our guard this day. Let every man
Bear a charged pistol hid, and, at a watch-word
Given by a musket, when our self sees time,
Rush in, and, if Medina's faction wrestle
Against your forces, kill, but if yield, save.
Be secret!

ALANZO
I am charmed, Sir.

Exit ALANZO.

KING
Watch Valasco.
If any wear a Cross, feather or glove,
Or such prodigious signs of a knit faction,
Table their names up. At our court-gate plant
Good strength to bar them out, if once they swarm.
Do this upon thy life.

VALASCO
Not death shall fright me.

Exit VALASCO and LOPEZ, enter BALTHAZAR.

BALTHAZAR
'Tis done, Sir.

KING
Death! What's Done?

BALTHAZAR
Young cub's flayed, but the she-fox shifting her hole is fled. The little jackanapes, the boy's brained.

KING
Sebastian?

BALTHAZAR
He shall ne'r speak more Spanish.

KING
Thou teachest me to curse thee.

BALTHAZAR
For a bargain you set your hand to.

KING
Half my crown I'd lose were it undone.

BALTHAZAR
But half a crown! That's nothing.
His brains stick in my conscience more than yours.

KING

How lost I the French doctor?

BALTHAZAR
As Frenchmen lose their hair. Here was too hot staying for him.

KING
Get thou from my sight, the Queen would see thee.

BALTHAZAR
Your gold, Sir.

KING
Go with Judas and repent.

BALTHAZAR
So men hate whores after lust's heat is spent.
I'm gone, Sir.

KING
Tell me true, is he dead?

BALTHAZAR
Dead.

KING
No matter. 'Tis but morning of revenge,
The sunset shall be red and tragical.

Exit KING.

BALTHAZAR
Sin is a raven croaking her own fall.

Exit BALTHAZAR.

SCENE II

Enter MEDINA, DAENIA, ALBA, CARLO and The Faction with Rosemary in their hats.

MEDINA
Keep locked the door, and let none enter to us
But who shares our fortunes.

DAENIA
Lock the doors.

ALBA
What entertainment did the King bestow
Upon your letters and the Cardinal's?

MEDINA
With a devouring eye he read them o'er,
Swallowing our offers into his empty bosom,
As gladly as the parched earth drinks healths
Out of the cup of heaven.

CARLO
Little suspecting
What dangers closely lie enambushed.

DAENIA
Let us not trust to that. There's in his breast
Both fox and lion, and both these beasts can bite.
We must not now behold the narrowest loop-hole,
But presently suspect a winged bullet
Flies whizzing by our ears.

MEDINA
For when I let
The plummet fall to sound his very soul
In his close-chamber, being French-Doctor like,
He to the Cardinal's ear sung sorcerous notes,
The burden of his song, to mine, was death,
Onaelia's murder, and Sebastian's.
And think you his voice alters now? 'Tis strange,
To see how brave this tyrant shows in court,
Throned like a god. Great men are pretty stars,
When his rays shine, wonder fills up all eyes
By sight of him, let him but once check sin,
About him round all cry, oh excellent King!
Oh Saint-like man! But, let this King retire
Into his closet to put off his robes,
He like a player leaves his part too.
Open his breast, and with a sunbeam search it,
There's no such man. This King of gilded clay,
Within is ugliness, lust, treachery,
And a base soul, though reared Colossus-like.

BALTHAZAR beats to come.

DAENIA
None till he speaks, and that we know his voice.
Who are you?

BALTHAZAR (within)
An honest house-keeper in Rosemary Lane too, if you dwell in the same parish.

MEDINA
Oh 'tis our honest soldier, give him entrance.

BALTHAZAR
Men show like coarses, for I meet few but are stuck with Rosemary. Every one asked me who was married today, and I told them Adultery and Repentance, and that Shame and a Hangman followed them to church.

MEDINA
There's but two parts to play, shame has done hers,
But execution must close up the scene,
And for that cause these sprigs are worn by all,
Bags of marriage, now of funeral,
For death this day turns courtier.

BALTHAZAR
Who must dance with him?

MEDINA
The King, and all that are our opposites.
That dart or this must fly into the court
Either to shoot this blazing star from Spain,
Or else so long to wrap him up in clouds,
Till all the fatal fires in him burn out,
Leaving his state and conscience clear from doubt
Of following uproars.

ALBA
Kill not, but surprise him.

CARLO
That's my voice still.

MEDINA
Thine, soldier?

BALTHAZAR
Oh, this colic of a kingdom, when the wind of treason gets amongst the small guts, what a rumbling and a roaring it keeps. And yet, make the best of it you can, it goes on stinking. Kill a King?

DAENIA
Why?

BALTHAZAR

If men should pull the sun out of heaven every time 'tis eclipsed, not all the wax nor tallow in Spain would serve to make us candles for one year.

MEDINA
No way to purge
The sick state, but by opening a vein.

BALTHAZAR
Is that your French physic? If every one of us should be whipped according to our faults, to be lashed at a cart's tail would be held but a flea biting.

Enter SIGNOR NO.

MEDINA whispers
What are you? Come from the King?

NO
No.

BALTHAZAR
No? More no's? I know him, let him enter.

MEDINA
Signor, I thank your kind intelligence,
The news long since was sent into our ears,
Yet we embrace your love, so fare you well.

CARLO
Will you smell to a sprig of rosemary?

NO
No.

BALTHAZAR
Will you be hanged?

NO
No.

BALTHAZAR
This is either Signor No, or no Signor.

MEDINA
He makes his love to us a warning piece
To arm ourselves against we come to court,
Because the guard is doubled.

ALL

Tush, we care not.

BALTHAZAR
If any here arms his hand to cut off the head, let him first pluck out my throat. In any noble act I'll wade chin-deep with you. But to kill a King?

MEDINA
No hear me...

BALTHAZAR
You were better, my Lord, sail five hundred times to Bantam in the West Indies, that once to Barathrum in the Low Countries. It's hot going under the line there, the calenture of the soul is a most miserable madness.

MEDINA
Turn then this wheel of fate from shedding blood
Till with her own hand Justice weighs all.

BALTHAZAR
Good.

Exeunt.

SCENE III

Enter QUEEN, MALATESTE.

QUEEN
Must then his trul be once more sphered in court
To triumph in my spoils, in my eclipses?
And I like moping Juno sit, whilst Jove
Varies his lust into five hundred shapes
To steal to his whore's bed! No Malateste,
Italian fires of Jealousy burn my marrow.
For to delude my hopes, the lecherous king
Cuts out this robe of cunning marriage,
To cover his incontinence, which flames
Hot, as my fury, in his black desires.
I am swollen big with child of vengeance now,
And till delivered, feel the throws of hell.

MALATESTE
Just is your imagination, high and noble,
And the brave heat of a true Florentine:
For Spain trumpets abroad her interest
In the King's heart, and with a black coal draws

On every wall your scoffed at injuries,
As one that has the refuse of her sheets,
And the sick Autumn of the weakened King,
Where she drunk pleasures up in the full spring.

QUEEN
That, Malateste, that, that torrent wracks me.
But Hymen's torch, held downward, shall drop out,
And for it, the mad Furies swing their brands
About the bride-chamber.

MALATESTE
The priest that joins them,
Our twin born malediction.

QUEEN
Loud it may speak.

MALATESTE
The herbs and flowers to strew the wedding way,
Be cypress, eugh, cold colliquintida.

QUEEN
Herbane and poppy, and that magical weed
Which hags at midnight watch to catch the seed.

MALATESTE
To these our execrations, and what mischief
Hell can but hatch in a distracted brain,
I'll be the executioner, though it look
So horrid it can fright even murder back.

QUEEN
Poison his whore today, for thou shalt wait
On the King's cup, and when heated with wine
He calls to drink the bride's health, marry her
Alive to a gaping grave.

MALATESTE
At board?

QUEEN
At board.

MALATESTE
When she being guarded round about with friends,
Like a fairy land, hemmed with rocks and seas,
What rescue shall I find?

QUEEN
Mine arms. Dost faint?
Stood all the Pyrenean hills that part
Spain and our country, on each others shoulders,
Burning with Aetnean flame, yet thou should'st on,
As being my steel of resolution,
First striking sparkles from my flinty breast.
Wert thou to catch the horses of the sun
Fast by their bridles, and to turn back day,
Would'st thou not do it, base coward, to make way
To the Italians second bliss, revenge?

MALATESTE
Were my bones threatened to the wheel of torture
I'll do it.

Enter LOPEZ.

QUEEN
A raven's voice, and it likes me well.

LOPEZ
The King expects your presence.

MALATESTE
So, so we come.
To turn this bride's day to a day of doom.

Exeunt.

SCENE IV

A banquet set out, cornets sounding; enter at one door, LOPEZ, VALASCO, ALANZO, NO. After them KING, CARDINAL, with DON COCKADILLIO, BRIDEGROOM, QUEEN and MALATESTE after. At the other door, ALBA, CARLO, RODERIGO, MEDINA and DAENIA leading ONAELIA as bride, CORNEGO, and JUANNA after, BALTHAZAR alone. The Bride and Bridegroom kiss, and by the CARDINAL are joined hand in hand. The KING is very merry, hugging MEDINA very lovingly.

KING
For half Spain's weigh in ingots I'd not lose
This little man today.

MEDINA
Not for so much
Twice told Sir, would I miss your Kingly presence.

Mine eyes have lost the acquaintance of your face
So long, and I so little late read o'er
That index of the royal book your mind,
That scarce, without your comment, can I tell
When in those leaves you turn o'er smiles or frowns.

KING
'Tis dimness of your sight, no fault i'the letter.
Medina, you shall find that free from erratas,
And for a proof, if I could breathe my heart
In welcome forth, this hall should ring naught else.
Welcome Medina, Good Marquis Daenia,
Dons of Spain all welcome.
My dearest love and Queen, be it your place
To entertain the bride, and do her grace.

QUEEN
With all the love I can, whose fire is such,
To give her heat, I cannot burn too much.

KING
Contracted bride, and bridegroom sit,
Sweet flowers not plucked in season lose their scent,
So will our pleasures. Father Cardinal,
Methinks this morning new begins our reign.

CARDINAL
Peace had her Sabbath ne'r till now in Spain.

KING
Where is our noble soldier Balthazar?
So close in conference with that Signor?

NO
No.

KING
What think'st thou of this great day Balthazar?

BALTHAZAR
Of this day? Why as of a new play, if it ends well, all's well. All but men are but actors, now if you being the King should be out of your part, or the Queen out of hers, or your Dons out if theirs, here's No will never be out of his.

NO
No.

BALTHAZAR

'Twere a lamentable piece of stuff to see great statesmen have vile exits, but I hope there are nothing but plaudities in all your eyes.

KING
Mine I protest are free.

QUEEN
And mine by heaven.

MALATESTE [Aside]
Free from one good look till the blow be given.

KING
Wine. A full cup crowned to Medina's health.

MEDINA
Your highness this day so much honours me,
That I to pay you what I truly owe,
My life shall venture for it.

DAENIA
So shall mine.

KING
Onaelia, you are sad. Why frowns your brow?

ONAELIA
A foolish memory of my past ills
Folds up my look in furrows of old care,
But my heart's merry, Sir.

KING
Which mirth to heighten,
Your bridegroom and yourself first pledge this health
Which we begin to our High Constable.

Three cups filled, one to the KING, the second to the BRIDEGROOM and the third to ONAELIA, with whom the KING compliments.

QUEEN
Is't speeding?

MALATESTE
As all our Spanish figs are.

KING
Here's to Medina's heart with all my heart.

MEDINA
My heart shall pledge your heart i'th deepest draught
That ever Spaniard drank.

KING
Medina mocks me,
Because I wrong her with the largest bowl.
I'll change with thee Onaelia.

MALATESTE rages.

QUEEN
Sir, you shall not!

KING
Fear you I cannot fetch it off?

QUEEN
Malateste!

KING
This is your scorn to her, because I am doing
This poorest honour to her. Music sound,
It goes were it ten fathoms to the ground.

Cornets play. KING drinks, QUEEN and MALATESTE storm.

MALATESTE
Fate strikes with the wrong weapon.

QUEEN
Sweet Royal Sir no more, it is too deep.

MALATESTE
Twill hurt your health sir.

KING
Interrupt me in my drink? 'Tis off.

MALATESTE
Alas Sir.
You have drunk your last, that poisoned bowl I filled
Not to be put in your hand, but hers.

KING
Poisoned?

ALL

Descend black speckled soul to hell!

[The faction turn on MALATESTE and wound him.]

MALATESTE
The Queen has sent me thither.

MALATESTE dies.

CARDINAL
What new fury shakes now with her snake's locks?

QUEEN
I, I, 'tis I
Whose soul is torn in pieces, till I send
This harlot home.

CARDINAL
More murders! Save the Lady.

BALTHAZAR
Rampant? Let the Constable make a mittimus.

MEDINA
Keep them asunder.

CARDINAL
How is it royal son?

KING
I feel no poison yet, only mine eyes
Are putting out their lights. Me thinks I feel
Death's icy fingers stroking down my face.
And now I'm in a mortal cold sweat.

QUEEN
Dear my Lord.

KING
Hence, call in my physicians.

MEDINA
Thy physician tyrant,
Dwells yonder, call on him or none.

KING
Bloody Medina, stab'st thou Brutus too?

DAENIA
As he is, so are we all.

KING
I burn,
My brains boil in a cauldron, oh one drop
Of water now to cool me.

ONAELIA
Oh, let him have physicians.

MEDINA
Keep her back.

KING
Physicians for my soul, I need none else.
You'll not deny me those. Oh holy father,
Is there no mercy hovering in a cloud
For me a miserable King so drenched
In perjury and murder?

CARDINAL
Oh Sir, great store.

KING
Come down, come quickly down.

CARDINAL
I'll forthwith send
For a grave Friar to be your confessor.

KING
Do, do.

CARDINAL
And he shall cure your wounded soul.
Fetch him good soldier.

BALTHAZAR
So good a work, I'll hasten.

[Exit BALTHAZAR.]

KING
Onaelia! Oh she's drowned in tears! Onaelia,
Let me not die unpardoned at thy hands.

Enter BALTHAZAR, SEBASTIAN as a Friar with others.

CARDINAL
Here comes a better surgeon.

SEBASTIAN
Hail my good son
I come to be thy ghostly father.

KING
Ha?
My child! 'Tis my Sebastian, or some spirit
Sent in his shape to fright me.

BALTHAZAR
'Tis no goblin, Sir, feel. Your own flesh and blood, and much younger than you though he be bald, and calls you son. Had I been as ready to have cut his sheep's throat, as you were to send him to the shambles, he had bleated no more. There's less chalk upon your score of sins by these round O'es.

KING
Oh my dull soul look up, thou art somewhat lighter.
Noble Medina, see Sebastian lives.
Onaelia cease to weep, Sebastian lives.
Fetch me my crown. My sweetest pretty Friar
Can my hands do't, I'll raise thee one step higher.
Thou'st been in heaven's house all this while sweet boy?

SEBASTIAN
I had but coarse cheer.

KING
Thou could'st n'er fare better.
Religious houses are those hives where bees
Make honey for men's souls. I tell thee boy,
A Friary is a cube, which strongly stands,
Fashioned by men, supported by heaven's hands.
Orders of holy priesthood are as high
I'th eyes of Angels, as a King's dignity.
Both these unto a Crown give the full weight,
And both are thine. You that our contract know,
See how I seal it with this marriage.
My blessing and Spain's kingdom both be thine.

ALL
Long live Sebastian.

ONAELIA
Doff that Friar's coarse grey.
And since he's crowned a King, clothe him like one.

KING
Oh no. Those are right sovereign ornaments.
Had I been clothed so, I had never filled
Spain's chronicle with my black calumny.
My work is almost finished. Where's my Queen?

QUEEN
Here piecemeal, torn by Furies.

KING
Onaelia!
Your hand Paulina too, Onaelia yours.
This hand, the pledge of my twice broken faith,
By you usurped is her inheritance.
My love is turned, see as my fate is turned,
Thus they today laugh, yesterday which mourned.
I pardon thee my death. Let her be sent
Back into Florence with a trebled dowry.
Death comes, oh now I see what late I feared!
A contract broke, though pieced up ne'r so well,
Heaven sees, earth suffers, but it ends in hell.

KING dies.

ONAELIA
Oh, I could die with him.

QUEEN
Since the bright sphere
I moved in falls, alas what make I here?

Exit QUEEN.

MEDINA
The hammers of black mischief now cease beating,
Yet some irons still are heating. You Sir Bridegroom,
Set all this while up as a mark to shoot at,
We here discharge you of your bedfellow,
She loves no barber's washing.

COCKADILLIO
My balls are saved then.

MEDINA
Be it your charge, so please you reverend Sir,
To see the late Queen safely to Florence.
My niece Onaelia, and that trusty soldier,

We do appoint to guard the infant King.
Other distractions, time must reconcile.
The State is poisoned like a crocodile.

Thomas Dekker – A Short Biography

Thomas Dekker was born around 1572, there is no certainty as to date and it is only probable that he was born in London. Little is known of his early years. From such an unknown start he was however to make quite a name for himself.

By the mid 1590s Dekker had set forth on a career as a playwright. Samples of his work (though not the actual date) can be found in the manuscript of Sir Thomas More. Of more certainty is work as a playwright for the Admiral's Men of Philip Henslowe, in whose records of account he is first mentioned in early 1598.

While there are plays connected with his name performed as early as 1594, it is not clear that he was the original author or part of a team involved in revising and updating. Much of his work has been lost and whilst his prolific output argues against any uniform quality there are undoubted gems both as a solo writer and as part of various collaborations. Indeed between 1598 and 1602, about forty plays for Henslowe, usually in collaboration, can be attributed to him.

Dekker's name first appears in Henslowe's diary* in connection with "fayeton" (presumably, Phaeton) in 1598. There follow, before 1599, payments for work on The Triplicity of Cuckolds, The Mad Man's Morris, and Hannibal and Hermes. He worked on these plays with Robert Wilson, Henry Chettle, and Michael Drayton. With Drayton, he also worked on history plays on the French civil wars, Earl Godwin, and others.

It is also recorded at this time that Dekker's long association with financial mishaps was going to be a life-long concern. He was imprisoned for a short time for debt in Poultry Compter, a small prison run by the Sherriff of London. It was used to house prisoners such as vagrants, debtors and religious dissenters, as well as criminals convicted of misdemeanours including homosexuality, prostitution and drunkenness.

In 1599, he wrote plays on Troilus and Cressida, Agamemnon (with Chettle), and Page of Plymouth. In that year, also, he collaborated with Chettle, Jonson, and Marston on a play about Robert II.

1599 also saw the production of three plays that have survived including his most famous work, The Shoemaker's Holiday, or the Gentle Craft. This play reflects the daily lives of ordinary Londoners, and contains the poem The Merry Month of May. The play reflects the trend for the intermingling of everyday subjects with the fantastical, embodied here by the rise of a craftsman to Mayor and the involvement of an unnamed but idealised king in the concluding banquet. Old Fortunatus and Patient Grissel are the two other surviving plays.

In 1600, he worked on The Seven Wise Masters, Fortune's Tennis, Cupid and Psyche, and Fair Constance of Rome. The next year, in addition to the classic Satiromastix, he worked on a play possibly about

Sebastian of Portugal and Blurt, Master Constable, on which he may have collaborated with Thomas Middleton.

To these years also belong the collaborations with Ben Jonson and John Marston, which presumably contributed to the War of the Theatres in 1600 and 1601. To Jonson, Dekker was a hack, a "dresser of plays about town"; Jonson made fun of Dekker as Demetrius Fannius in Poetaster and as Anaides in Cynthia's Revels.

Dekker's riposte, Satiromastix, performed both by the Lord Chamberlain's Men and the child actors of Paul's, casts Jonson as an affected, hypocritical Horace and marks the end of the "poetomachia".

In 1602 he revised two older plays, Pontius Pilate (1597) and the second part of Sir John Oldcastle. He also collaborated on Caesar's Fall, Jephthah, A Medicine for a Curst Wife, Sir Thomas Wyatt (on Wyatt's rebellion), and Christmas Comes But Once a Year.

By 1603, Jonson and Dekker collaborated again, on a pageant for the Royal Entry, delayed from the coronation of James I, for which Dekker also wrote the festival book The Magnificent Entertainment.

At this point Dekker becomes more interested in writing pamphlets; he had done so from the start of his career but now increases his work flow and his playwriting output noticeably declines. It appears also that his association with Henslowe also breaks at this point.

In Dekker's first rush of pamphleteering, in 1603, was The Wonderful Year, a journalistic account of the death of Elizabeth, accession of James I, and the 1603 plague, that combined a wide variety of literary styles to convey the extraordinary events of that year ('wonderful' here meaning astonishing). Its reception prompted two more plague pamphlets, News From Gravesend and The Meeting of Gallants at an Ordinary. The Double PP (1606) is an anti-Catholic tract written in response to the Gunpowder Plot. News From Hell (1606) is an homage to and continuation of Nash's Pierce Penniless. The Seven Deadly Sins of London (1606) continues the plague pamphlet series.

In 1604, he and Middleton wrote The Honest Whore for the Fortune, and Dekker contributed a sequel himself the following year. The Middleton/Dekker collaboration The Family of Love also dates from this time. Dekker and Webster also wrote Westward Ho and Northward Ho for Paul's Boys.

The failures of The Whore of Babylon (1607) and If This Be Not a Good Play, the Devil is in It (1611) left him crestfallen; the latter play was rejected by Prince Henry's Men before failing for Queen Anne's Men at the Red Bull Theatre.

After 1608, Dekker produced his most popular pamphlets: a series of "cony-catching" pamphlets that described the various tricks and deceits of confidence-men and thieves, including Thieves' Cant. These pamphlets, which Dekker often updated and reissued, include The Belman of London (1608, now The Bellman of London), Lanthorne and Candle-light, Villainies Discovered by Candlelight, and English Villainies. They owe their form and many of their incidents to similar pamphlets by Robert Greene.

Other pamphlets are journalistic in form and offer vivid pictures of Jacobean London. The Dead Term (1608) describes Westminster during summer vacation. The Guls Horne-Booke (1609, now The Gull's Hornbook) describes the life of city gallants, with a valuable account of behaviour in the London theatres. Work for Armourers (1609) and The Artillery Garden (1616) (the latter in verse) describe aspects of England's military industries. London Look Back (1630) treats 1625, the year of James's death, while Wars, Wars, Wars (1628) describes European turmoil.

The Roaring Girl, a city comedy that using the real-life figure 'Moll Cutpurse', aka Mary Frith, was another collaboration with Middleton in 1611. The same year, he wrote another tragicomedy; Match Me in London.

In 1612, Dekker's lifelong problem with debt reached a crisis point when he was imprisoned in the King's Bench Prison on a debt of forty pounds to the father of John Webster. He remained there for seven years and continued writing pamphlets during these years but wrote no plays. He did however contribute six prison-based sketches to the sixth edition (1616) of Sir Thomas Overbury's Characters; and he revised Lanthorne and Candlelight to reflect what he had learned in prison.

Dekker also wrote a long poem Dekker His Dreame (1620) cataloguing his despairing confinement;

After his release, he collaborated with Day on Guy of Warwick (1620), The Wonder of a Kingdom (1623), and The Bellman of Paris (1623). He also wrote the tragicomedy The Noble Spanish Soldier (1622) and later reworked material from this play into a comedic form to produce The Welsh Ambassador (1623).

With John Ford, he wrote The Sun's Darling (1624), The Fairy Knight (1624), and The Bristow Merchant (1624).

Another play, The Late Murder of the Son upon the Mother, or Keep the Widow Waking (with Ford, Webster, and William Rowley) dramatized two recent murders in Whitechapel, and resulted in a suit for slander heard in the Star Chamber.

Dekker turned once more to pamphlet-writing, revamping old work and writing a new preface to his most popular tract, The Bellman of London.

Dekker's plays of the 1620s were staged at the large amphitheaters on the north side of London, most commonly at the Red Bull; only two of his later plays were seen at the more exclusive, indoor Cockpit Theatre. The Shoreditch amphitheaters had become identified with the louder, less reputable play-goers, such as apprentices. Dekker's type of play seems to have suited them perfectly. Full of bold action and complementary to the values and beliefs of such audiences, his drama carried much of the thrusting optimism of Elizabethan drama into the Caroline era.

Dekker published no more work after 1632, and he it is thought he died on August 25th, 1632, recorded as "Thomas Dekker, householder". He is buried at St. James's in Clerkenwell.

Most of Dekker's work is lost. His disordered life, and his lack of a firm connection (such as Shakespeare had) with a single company, may have hindered the preservation or publication of manuscripts although perhaps twenty of his plays were published during his lifetime.

Henslowe's diary
Philip Henslowe was an Elizabethan theatrical entrepreneur and impresario although he had a wide range of other business interests. Henslowe's reputation rests on the survival of his diary, a primary source for information about the theatrical world of Renaissance London.

Henslowe's "diary" is a valuable source on the theatrical history of the period. It is a collection of memoranda and notes that record payments to writers, box office takings, and lists of money lent. Also of interest are records of the purchase of expensive costumes and of stage properties, such as the dragon in Christopher Marlowe's Doctor Faustus, providing an insight into the staging of plays in the Elizabethan theatre.

The diary is written on the reverse of pages of a book of accounts of his brother-in-law Ralf Hogge's ironworks, kept by his brother John Henslowe for the period 1576–1581. Hogge was the Queen's Gunstone maker, and produced both iron cannon and shot for the Royal Armouries at the Tower of London. John Henslowe seems to have acted as his agent, and Philip to have prudently reused his old account book. Hence these entries are also a valuable source for the early iron-making industry.

The diary begins with Henslowe's theatrical activities for 1592. Entries, with varying degrees of detail (authors' names were not included before 1597), until 1609. In the years before his death, Henslowe appears to have run his theatrical interests from a greater distance.

The diary records payments to twenty-seven Elizabethan playwrights. He variously commissioned, bought and produced plays by, or made loans to Ben Jonson, Christopher Marlowe, Thomas Middleton, Robert Greene, Henry Chettle, George Chapman, Thomas Dekker, John Webster, Anthony Munday, Henry Porter, John Day, John Marston and Michael Drayton. The diary reveals the varying partnerships between writers, in an age when many plays were collaborations. It also shows Henslowe to have been a careful man of business, obtaining security in the form of rights to his authors' works, and holding their manuscripts, while tying them to him with loans and advances. If a play was successful, Henslowe would commission a sequel.

Performances of works with titles similar to Shakespearean plays, such as a Hamlet, a Henry VI, Part 1, a Henry V, a The Taming of the Shrew and a Titus Andronicus are mentioned in the diary with no author listed. Most of these plays were recorded when the Admiral's Men and the Lord Chamberlain's Men briefly joined forces when the playhouses were closed owing to the plague (June 1594).

In 1599, Henslowe paid Dekker and Henry Chettle for a play called Troilus and Cressida, which is probably the play currently known as British Museum MS. Add 10449 (the actors' names that appear in the plot connect it to the Admiral's Men and date it between March 1598 and July 1600). There is no mention of William Shakespeare (or for that matter Richard Burbage) in Henslowe's diary (despite the forgeries of John Payne Collier), this is due to the fact that Shakespeare and Burbage were during most of their career not connected to Henslowe's theatre, Shakespeare's company, the Lord Chamberlain's Men, performed at The Theatre (starting in 1594) and later The Globe Theatre (starting in 1599).

Thomas Dekker – A Concise Bibliography

Plays – Sole Authorship
The Shoemaker's Holiday (1599)
Old Fortunatus (1600)
The Noble Spanish Soldier (1602)
Troja-Nova Triumphans, or London Triumphing (1612)
London's Tempe; or, The Feild of Happines (1629)

The Honest Whore, Part II (1630)
Match Me in London (1631)
The Wonder of a Kingdom (1634)

Plays – Co-Written
Satiro-Mastix (1601) with Marston
Blurt, Master Constable (1602) with Middleton
Patient Grissill (1603) with Chettle and Haughton
The Honest Whore, Part I (1604) with Middleton
The Magnificent Entertainment (1604) with Jonson et al.
The Family of Love (1603-1607) with Middleton
Northward Ho (1607) with Webster
Westward Ho (1607) with Webster
The Famous History of Sir Thomas Wyatt (1607) with Webster
The Roaring Girl (1610) with Middleton
The Witch of Edmonton (1621) with Ford, Rowley, &c.
The Virgin-Martyr (1622) with Massinger
The Sun's Darling (1623-4) with Ford
The Bloody Banquet (1639) with Middleton

Non-Dramatic Works
The Wonderful Year (1603)
News from Hell (1606)
The Double PP (1606)
The Seven Deadly Sins of London (1606)
Jests to Make You Merry (1607)
The Bellman of London (1608)
Lanthorne and Candle-light (1608)
The Dead Term (1608)
The Gull's Hornbook (1609)
The Four Birds of Noah's Ark (1609)
The Raven's Almanack (1609)
Work for Armourers (1609)
O Per Se O (1612)
A Strange Horse-Race (1613)
Dekker, His Dreame (1620)
A Rod for Runaways (1625)

Poems
Golden Slumbers Kiss Your Eyes
Beauty Arise
Cast Away Care
The Invitation
Fancies Are But Streams
Here Lies The Blithe Spring

www.ingramcontent.com/pod-product-compliance
Lightning Source LLC
Chambersburg PA
CBHW071325040426

42444CB00009B/2082